Introduction

How would you like to give yourself a six-figure raise, boost your brand awareness, drive new customers in your doors, and kick your competitors asses?

It should be obvious by now that you need a strong social media presence- but you would be surprised how many bar & restaurant owners have ignored the impact social media can have on their bottom line. Many know deep down that the 'eyeballs', or potential customers are on social media.

But HOW do you optimize your pages, engage your customers, automate processes, and ultimately cash in with your businesses social media presence? You need to arm yourself with more knowledge and know-how than your competitors. **You can't wait another day**- start employing the strategies I have laid out in this book and start dominating your competition.

So who is **Ryan Gougeon** (*pronounced Gou-Zheon*) and why the hell should you listen to me?

For starters, I've gotten International media exposure in thousands of news outlets, newspapers, blogs you name it- more than once and for different stunts.

I used Social Media as my base to get that attention.

That's right, millions of dollars in free advertising for my brands by utilizing Social Media. My bar & restaurant has won Tampa Bay Times prestigious "Ultimate Bar" award the past 8 consecutive years in a row, an award given to only 40 bars & restaurants out of over 2,000 in the Tampa Bay area.

My restaurants have won numerous culinary awards, awards from Guinness Corporation, numerous "Best Of The Bay" awards, and many more. Many people refer to me as "The next P.T. Barnum", which I consider one of the highest compliments a marketer could receive.

But enough about me. If you want to know more, you can head over to my website, www.BarRestaurantguru.com.

What you'll learn in this book

In this book, I'll show you how to utilize all the major social media sites to your advantage. Think of it as learning how to build nukes while your competitors are still trying to figure out how to use gun powder. You'll have an unfair advantage by learning social media etiquette, tactics, strategies, special tools to automate posting, do's and don'ts, and much, much more. This book was laid out so that the complete novice or experienced Social Media marketer can benefit from it.

HOW to use this book

If you aren't adept at Social Media just yet, don't worry. Each chapter is broken down into dealing with one platform at a time. The key is to build up one or two platforms at a time, optimize those platforms, and then interact with customers and build your user base.

While I recommend reading it cover to cover *twice* and making notes, feel free to skip to the chapters you find most useful.

If you were to ask me, I'd advise a client to optimize and make these three hot, in this order:

1. Facebook
2. Instagram

3. Google+ (Google My Business page, claim your businesses page ASAP if you have not already!)
   After you make these three red hot you can move on to other platforms. The more platforms you have a great presence on, the higher your ranking with the search engines, and the more reach you'll have with potential customers.

   Just remember- your competitors are either getting drunk right now or sleeping- while you have the fucking nuke codes in your hand.

   Read this book twice before emailing me with questions. I will help answer any questions you have. Between this book and me helping you, the only thing standing in the way right now between you and a six figure raise- is *you*.

   Swing for the fences,

   -Ryan Gougeon

   For downloads, tips, tricks, videos, and help, visit my site at:
   www.BarRestaurantGuru.com

 Ryan Gougeon

Contents

Bars, Restaurants, and Nightclubs

"If your social media pages aren't making you money, you are about to give yourself a six figure raise by reading my book"-Ryan Gougeon

There is a point in everyone's life when they say "What the hell, I should start a bar/restaurant." And they never do. You did do it however, and now you know why a lot of people don't go through with it. Being your own boss is rewarding, but tough. Owning your own establishment is equal parts headache and exhilaration. This book is designed to take some of the headache, heartache, and guesswork out of starting your own social media marketing campaign for your bar, restaurant, or nightclub.

If you're fortunate enough to be able to hire a social media director or someone to do the legwork for you, first of all congratulations. Secondly, this book will act as a primer to allow you to have a better grasp of what should be happening within your social media campaign and the direction it should be headed.

Unfortunately there are quite a few people out there who claim to be social media specialists or experts. Many, if not most of them are legitimate consultants, professionals who do in fact have a marketing background and understand how to leverage the social media environment to produce results for your business.

That leaves us with the ones who aren't professionals and who aren't going to provide considerable value for your business. Understanding the basics (and then some) of the social media marketing process will help protect you and your resources from freelancers who may not produce the results they promise. And at the end of the day, the more you know about the process the more inclined you'll be to save your money and just run the campaign yourself using automated tools, like Buffer. You've gotten this far on your own haven't you?

One of the most important things to remember about starting a social media campaign for your business is that it is not a one foot in the water

An effective social media campaign requires effort, management, and planning. Understanding this is the first step to differentiating yourself from the competition.

endeavor; both feet have to get wet. This means

understanding that just like any other business undertaking, a social media campaign requires effort, management, and planning. This is crucial to the success of any program and you will see this point stressed many times over throughout this book.

Understanding this characteristic of social media campaigns alone puts you ahead of your competitors who say "Yes, we do have a social media campaign, you can find us on Facebook where we have a business page". A single Facebook page a social media campaign does not make; more on that later. This point also will help you separate potentially productive social media directors from downright lousy ones.

A social media marketing campaign isn't a magic pill. It alone won't save an establishment that is poorly run, mismanaged, or on its way out. Any marketing campaign needs to be backed up by a solid product, which in this case is your food, drinks, atmosphere, and environment. You've worked hard to turn your business into the establishment it is today, and the first step in all of this is to make sure you have everything in order.

Jon Taffer of Spike TV's *Bar Rescue* says "When my company does a good job we make people happy. They laugh, they smile, and they have a good time – that's what we do for a living. Any business doing that is making a noble effort."

Taffer goes on to talk about some of the goals and the ways he views traffic-based businesses like bars, restaurants, and clubs in an article for Entrepreneur[1]. Having a strong understanding of the business that you

---

[1] Source: Entrepreneur Oct. 4, 2013 "10 Things Jon Taffer of 'Bar Rescue' Wants You to Know About Running a Business" by Ashley Lee

are in and how it grows will help you make the best decisions when the time comes to start evaluating your social media marketing campaign.

Ensuring that every customer who enters your establishment has a positive experience is crucial. The exact nature of engineering positive customer experiences varies based on a number of factors such as locale, demographics, business model, and brand perception, but there are a few basic commonalities.

A great experience once is great, but a consistently great experience often is much, much better. An average standard in the world of commerce is the calculation that it costs businesses 3 to 5 times more to attract new customers than it does do keep existing customers happy. This number may be skewed slightly lower for local bars and restaurants but the fact remains that the best customers are repeat customers. A consistent experience that meets or exceeds your customers' expectations is the key to building a long-lasting and valuable brand.

Taffer puts it this way: out of all the customers that visit your establishment (bar, eatery, café,) fewer than half will return. This is not because your establishment is the worst in town, but because visiting your business is still outside their habit cycle. Of those that do patronize your business again, 50% of those customers will return. That sounds depressing, but if they visit a third time, over 70% of those customers will continue to return. It is for this reason that first impressions are just as important as third, fourth, and fifth impressions. Consistency and predictability will entice customers to become the best kind of customers (repeat customers) and will make your business easier to monitor and plan.

> Over time the stakes are high to retain customers. Crafting a consistent and predictable experience will help keep customers coming back and will develop loyalty and value for your brand.

Staff are also an integral part of your customers' experience. Hiring for experience is a smart business decision, but understanding the role that attitude plays in making or breaking a customer's experience is vital. A host or bartender with over a decade experience will certainly be a knowledgeable asset, but if that person is surly and generates complaints then the situation must be rectified. A new employee with the right attitude and mentality can be coached to be a professional whereas in some cases a professional with a bad attitude can become deadweight for your business with no improvement on the horizon. Of course these are general terms; the circumstance changes with each person concerned. Managing people and staffing your business is certainly one of the hardest and continually changing aspects of running a bar or restaurant but you couldn't be where you are without your people. Unless of course you can do it all yourself, but who wants to do that?

Your team is integral to your business and it is important to remember that you are running a business. Underperforming or weak employees shouldn't be coddled or protected. With all new employees there is a certain amount of time they will need to become acclimated, and everyone slips up every once in a while. With this in mind, it is important to remember that weak links in your businesses chain can impact your profits and your bottom line. Strong performers should be encouraged and pushed while those who struggle may need more attention. Inevitably, if their performance within the workplace is a drain, and not an asset, choices that can sometimes be tough must be made.

This can sometimes mean throwing training out the window in favor of teaching. Training is 'behavior modification" and this process takes time and resources. Training may be necessary for janitorial staff or kitchen staff and bartenders but the method of teaching these employees favors giving them the tools and direction they need along with encouragement to produce their own results. You spent a long time and a lot of hard work to bring your business to the point it's at now. Relax, hire people with the right skills and attitude and let them drive the business. Your people will be happier, you'll be happier, and you may even learn a thing or two. Just don't be afraid to step in when the situation calls for it.

Ultimately you know your customers, your business, and your target demographic. A common theme in this book is delivering the knowledge you need to make informed decisions about the direction of your business, your social media campaign, and your brand. Just like repeat customers being the best kind of customers, informed decisions are the best kind of decisions. Whenever you are called upon to make a business decision it is essential to ask yourself a few key questions.

- How will the outcome of this decision affect the direction of my brand? Is that outcome in line with the long-term vision I have for my business?

- Will this business decision have an impact on the experience I provide to my customers? Will it improve that experience? Can these improvements be maintained on a consistent basis?

- Am I setting realistic expectations for the outcomes of this decision?

Later in this book we discuss the S.M.A.R.T. method of setting goals which is a great way to analyze how realistic your plans are and to effectively set goals, whether making decisions for your social media campaign or within the setting of your overall business.

Before we get started with the nuts and bolts of building your social media campaign, let's take a look at how marketing works in principle and how the social media environment came about. It is important to understand the marketing environment and the advent of social media in order to effectively leverage those capabilities and to understand the direction that social networking services are taking.

Let's get started.

A Crash Course in Marketing

from traditional to contemporary

When we examine marketing in the context of social media we must first examine traditional methods of marketing. The answer to the question "what is marketing?" is both simple and complex. Simply put, marketing is defined as follows.

Marketing is the action or business of promoting and selling products or services, including market research and advertising.

This is a good description for an entry in a dictionary and it was reached through a simple Google search. But what makes a good dictionary definition may not help us produce something actionable and may not even be that enlightening at all. This simple definition, while being technically correct, is not all that helpful.

Contemporary marketing is best seen as a dialogue. This definition of marketing takes quite a bit more explaining and a look back at the manner in which contemporary marketing came about but it expands the concept of applied marketing from simple TV ads and billboards to the exchange of information that it is today. This definition also demonstrates how the current social media marketing environment is the logical conclusion of a long chain of marketing-world events paired with the advancement of global technology.

> Marketing is not simply the promotion of products by companies to customers. It has evolved into a dialogue between buyer and seller where both parties have a voice.

Marketing is a dialogue between a company and their customer and with the advent of social media that dialogue is changing and evolving rapidly. Marketing is only now a dialogue; it traditionally has been a very one-sided conversation. That is to say that the voice that was speaking has, up until very recently, been that of the company and not of the customer. Traditional marketing in the context of a conversation can be considered a monologue because while companies were speaking, the voice of the customer was silent.

For quite a long time companies were satisfied generating products that they wanted to produce. This is vastly different from companies producing products that their customers wanted them to produce, a circumstance that modern companies are more familiar with today. Henry Ford famously said that the Model T automobile was available in any color the customer wanted as long as that color was black. That is certainly a far cry from the product differentiation that consumers today enjoy but it underscores the idea that the company (Ford Motorcar in this instance) produced goods as it saw fit and in a manner that was economical to the needs of the business. At that time, marketing was solely the act of making consumers aware of your product and outlining the features and benefits.

The marketing mix (often called the four P's of marketing) reflects the dialogue nature of the marketing process. Here we see marketing as a proxy for dialogue but not a true conversation. Marketing becomes the flow of information between the customer and the company. The customer's voice is represented with customer surveys, polls, and buying habits. Preferences are sampled through test groups and data begins to determine the direction that companies' production takes.

The four P's of marketing

- Product
- Price
- Place
- Promotion

Though the marketing mix is the product of what could be considered traditional marketing, the four P's are a powerful and lasting concept that can be applied to today's social media marketing environment.

Product, the first 'P', is a tangible good or an intangible service. In the context of this book, the bar and restaurant industry, our product is a combination of food, drinks, service, and atmosphere. This is not a book about how to run a successful bar or how to entice patrons to come back often and spend more money however, and the 'product' specifics are up to you. It is important to note that as your social media campaign develops (we'll be covering this in later chapters) if customer demand demonstrates changes that should be made to your 'product' a good move is to consider those requests.

Price, the second 'P' is always a consideration for you, your customers and your competition. As a decision maker for your business you understand how your price impacts your customers, your profits, and your competitive ability.

The third 'P', place, is the placement or distribution of your product. In this instance, the place is your establishment(s) where customers come to enjoy themselves. We can only assume that you have a killer location for your bar or restaurant. With a service based business, the concept of place becomes very one-dimensional. There are of course a multitude of other metrics to measure your business and encourage profitable behavior but they are beyond the scope of this book.

Promotion, the fourth 'P', is the subject of this book. Traditionally, promotion has existed as television ads, direct mailings, telephone marketing, print advertisements, billboards, etc... This aim of this book is not to tell you to discontinue using those methods; if you are tracking a positive return on investment than that method should continue to be employed, simple as that.

Promotion has seen a variety of different masters. Ad agencies gave way to marketing firms who lost control of advertising when corporations realized that they could do just as good a job as many of the marketing firms. But all of that is more or less out the window now; the consumer is the one who controls the face of advertising now.

As we examine in the next chapter, the days of T.V. ads are numbered as more and more consumers are taking advantage of their place within the conversation. Never before has the consumer had more control of the products and services that are offered and never before have companies been listening more attentively.

The Great
Democratizer

social media and the Internet

It is certainly no secret that the Internet has changed the way that we do pretty much everything. It is also no secret that we are still developing ways to utilize the World Wide Web and to leverage the totality of its business enhancing capacity. Statistica[2] estimates the number of internet users worldwide in 2016 at 2.92 billion. This number is up from 2.71 billion in 2015. Among the myriad of conditions and situations this has generated it has also given a large portion of these people a voice.

Through the natural course of business development companies have been determining that the needs of the customer are paramount to business success. Nowhere is this more evident than in the food service and restaurant industry. More and more have the goals of businesses been customer-aligned and marketing campaigns have also reflected this change.

A Primer on Social Media

Before we get started putting together some social media action plans and developing the foundations for social media marketing campaigns, we will cover a brief overview

---

[2] www.statistica.com/statistics accessed May 12, 2015

of social media specific terms and touch upon of the most common platforms. A platform, in the jargon of the social media industry, is the technological foundation for a social media channel. For example, Facebook is a platform. It is a software and browser environment through which users interact with one another.

A channel is the specific avenue used to create a connection and a dialogue with a customer. Continuing the example of Facebook, this would be your business' profile page. Channels do the work, platforms are the environment in which the work is done. The exact nature of the work depends on the channel, and the channel depends on the platform. For example, the method of conveyance used on the video-sharing platform YouTube is radically different than the photo-sharing service Flickr. The term for a social media channel is not unique to social media; traditional marketing has always referred to the specific methods of communicating with the customer as channels. This is an important concept as it highlights the fact that your social media campaign is a part of your overall marketing strategy.

When discussing social media, the term user describes the people who visit different channels across different platforms every day. Users often have accounts or profiles with their social media platform (or platforms) of choice. Different platforms or social media services use different names for the collection of information associated with each user that identifies and allows them to access content within a platform but for the sake of simplicity we will refer to them here as accounts or profiles.

A great feature of social media services is their established user base. Companies like Facebook, Twitter, and Tumblr have already put in the time to make their platforms appealing to users. People are already logging on and consuming social media services voraciously; as a business you are potentially given thousands upon thousands of sets of electronic ears to hear what you have to say. This is an optimistic view of the social media environment for businesses because while the ears are there, you do have to fight to be heard.

Social media, the democratization of consumers, and the rich exchange of ideas exists in a new Internet concept. Known as Web 2.0, this new web environment is characterized by a shift from static webpages to dynamic and user-generated content. Social media plays a huge role in what we know as Web 2.0. There is no bigger culprit than social media services such as Facebook and YouTube in regards to the vast amounts of user-generated content that has proliferated across the Internet.

Your Social Media Marketing Campaign

Any business undertaking needs to have goals. When you were securing funding from investors for your bar or restaurant it was necessary to draw up a business plan that outline goals and the means for achieving them and the undertaking of a social media campaign is no different. It is easy to assume that because your business has a Facebook page that is updated monthly that you have a social media campaign. Based on what we have covered already, no one who has read this far should still think that.

It is very important to identify exactly what you want your social media campaign to do for your business. Of course the end goal is to recover your investment and generate revenue but in the meantime specific goals focus your efforts and provide a baseline against which to scale measurements. Measurements are an essential part of maintaining a social media campaign. Without measurements of effectiveness you will have no idea what is working and what isn't or if you have made your money back or not. It is in this spirit that the goals you establish

- **Specific**

- **Measurable**

- **Acheivable**

- **Realistic**

- **Time-based**

for your social media campaign should be S.M.A.R.T.

The concept of smart goals is not unique to any industry or discipline; rather smart planning is the foundational basis for a wide variety of planning activities. Smart goals even transcend the world of commerce and are used by personal trainers and life coaches in the day to day lives of their clients.

Using the S.M.A.R.T. method to develop goals is, well, smart. But what should those goals look like, and what is a reasonable expectation from your social media presence. We know social media can't make your drinks cheaper or your food taste better so your goals should reflect what it can do. The following are some sample goals that relevant and realistic given social media's capacities and functions.

1. Increase the average check amount by 10% through coupon incentives and new cocktail and entrée exposure over the next four months.

2. Increase positive brand perception through positive reviews. This is intended to increase traffic by 10%

3. Attract 40 new website visits per week.

4. Capture 100 new email addresses per month.

These goals conform to the S.M.A.R.T method of effective goal setting and set a great initial hurdle. Of course as your business changes, your social media presence changes, or you meet your goals it will become necessary to revisit and rewrite these goals. It is shortsighted to rely on goals that are written in stone.

Your goals are also important to your campaign in another way too: identifying your ROI (return on investment). Like we mentioned in the previous chapter's marketing overview, understanding what your return on investment is for your social media campaign is crucial to understanding which efforts are working, which are dead weight, and where to focus your resources.

The biggest thing you should be aware of when undertaking a social media marketing campaign is the time commitment associated with social media success. Some social media channels can require daily interaction, multiple times a day. There are tools to help you do this, but as you read through this book and we cover each major social media platform it becomes rapidly clear that while social media services are generally free, the time investment required can quickly become massive.

> Committing to a social media campaign without the time to correctly administer it is setting yourself up for failure.

I don't know how to make that any clearer. Without the time to correctly administer a social media campaign you will not meet your goals and at best your efforts will be wasted. At worst, your brand's reputation could suffer.

If you can afford to hire or develop a social media director, great. There are also services that will run your campaign for you. If you're set on running it yourself, later in the book we'll talk about how to prioritize the services you should be using and how to budget your time. Additionally, we will cover the scheduling capacity of some of the major services that will allow you to "set and forget" posts and tweets which will save valuable time administering your campaign.

Your Website

Starting a social media marketing campaign without your own website is only going halfway with leveraging the social media experience for your brand (and your bottom line). Creating your own website is as easy as it is essential, even if you don't have any coding experience. There are hordes of programmers and code writers out there that are more than willing to produce just about any professional website that you could desire. Paying a dedicated programmer can get pricey though and a multitude of programs exist that do the work for you. For a fee the programs simplify the site design process and provide templates that allow you to drag and drop content into premade templates. For those interested in experimenting with easy to customize templates, this author recommends WordPress as a free-to-start business page template. As your presence grows, WordPress offers the option to upgrade to newer and more powerful options for your business that can scale with your needs.

Learning to code and producing the site yourself is the cheapest (and most challenging) path, but many web designers will tell you that code is easy enough to learn for those who are persistent. While coding is a great skill to know, the time needed to learn the necessary skills is often out of reach for many business owners.

Chances are better than not that you already have a website for your business. That's great, because your website will do a lot of things for your business and many of your social media channels will act as funnels for users, sending them all to your website (which should be designed as a funnel to send customers to your business). What makes an effective website for a bar or restaurant? Please ask *that* question and not "I serve beers, why does my establishment need a website?"

To be fair, there are certainly some places that don't have a website and don't need one (in their opinion). The decision makers at these establishments have traded exposure and accessibility for something else, usually a dedicated customer base or an atmosphere. That's fine as long as these owners and managers understand that this is a trade-off. If your competition has a website, you better have one as well. And if you're saying "There's no one like me in my city, I don't have any competition" that's not true.

While it may be true that there are no other establishments like yours you do compete. Diners have options. In a perfect world they would patronize your business every night. But people don't want the same food all of the time, even if you have a great rotational menu. You compete with every other place where diners can grab a bite to eat. Every time they make food for themselves at home, that's a lost sale for you, so you also indirectly compete with grocery stores as well.

Not a mile from where I sit typing this, there is an "underground" bar that fashions itself to be a Prohibition-era speakeasy. The theme is so strong that prospective patrons knock on an unmarked door and request tables from a hostess who does not admit that the business is actually a bar. Once inside, cellphones are strictly banned and it seems like all of the patrons and staff know one another at the cash-only bar. This place has a website. It is a landing page occupied by an antique gas lamp. Clicking on the flame of the lamp brings up a field allowing you to reserve space at the bar or in the lounge area. A place that bans cellphones has a website. Think about that.

While this is certainly a creative example of a business carving out a specific niche and (somewhat counterintuitively) relying on a website to drive reservations it is not particularly instructive for your business. So let's cover some of the essentials.

#1

Your website should be mobile optimized. We discuss the trend of smart device access to social media throughout this book and your website will be no different. Especially if your social media campaign funnels your fans, followers, and friends to your website. If they were on their phone looking at your Facebook page, they're not going to run home to bring up your website on their home computer.

#2

Your website should be easily updated. You will need to update information regarding specials, events, and seasonal or rotational menu items. When building the site in the beginning it is helpful to plan for this eventuality and many plug and play systems exist that make modifying your site's content easy. Later in this book we also discuss similar tools that simplify posting and tracking across all of your social media channels.

#3

Your website should support your social media campaign. It should support the campaign just as much as the campaign supports the site. Embed YouTube videos, Instagram photos, screenshots of tweets, whatever you do that builds your brand and reaches out to your customers. Using your social media campaign to reach your customers and grow your business is the topic of this book so you'll see more on all of that in the coming chapters.

#4

Support online reservations. It seems as though more and more people are hesitant to pick up the phone. Online bookings mean that your customers that are already probably using their phone to browse social media can quickly and easily reserve space at your business. In the event of a holiday or other high-traffic, high-seating day, your customers will automatically be refused a reservation, saving them the frustration of a trip to your packed restaurant only to be turned away. Of course a call would have sufficed, but they can't be bothered.

#5

Monitor your web traffic with analytics. There are a million analytics programs available and some hosting services provide rudimentary information as well. Template-based sites like WordPress come with built in analytics. Use analytics to gauge the effectiveness of programs like Instagram or Facebook contests and see which tactics work and which could use improvement.

#6

Your website should be a resource for your brand's reputation management. Did you get a good review on Yelp? or Google? Did someone publicly comment on the quality of your service? Links, embeds, or screenshots relating to these positive reviews can showcase the fruits of your hard labor and build your brand's reputation. Drop in forums can be helpful too to encourage conversation about your business but be prepared to respond in a timely manner to negative

comments.

#7

Any business website, not just those supporting a restaurant or bar, should have a solid **SEO** element. **SEO** stands for Search Engine Optimization, the term for the steps one takes to get their page to show up in search results reliably, and near the top of the results. In our Google Places chapter of this book we discuss some methods to outrank your competition in Google searches but the first step is to not just maintain a website with pictures and hours of operation, but with keyword-containing content as well as presence in multiple directories. Ensuring that your webpage has a description and title explicitly outlined within the html code will also result in higher search results placement.

#8

Harnessing the power of email marketing or "email blasts" through your website is a must to create the total Web 2.0 marketing package. On your website, through your social media channels, and through your traditional marketing channels as part of your marketing campaign encourage users to sign up for your mailing list. What they get is coupons, promotions, advance notice of events, and relevant articles. What you get is another touch point with your customers and an opportunity to remind them that you're the best place to eat in town.

When customers click the relevant link from your Facebook page, YouTube channel, Tweet, or insert social media channel here, they are brought to what is called a "squeeze page". A squeeze page has exactly one function: to collect your customers' email information. It should only have the relevant fields of name, email, and possibly zip code. Zip code is important to collect because that will help you identify where your business is coming from. If your squeeze page is littered with links or other distractors, you could lose sign-ups. Squeeze pages should always be all business.

Now that you have your customers' info, use a program like MailChimp (free for your first 2,000 subscribers) to send emails to your customers with all the things you promised them. Remember to comply with SPAM ACT guidelines and allow your customers to opt-out or discontinue your emails. In the same vein, your customers trusted you with their email addresses. Don't violate that trust by selling their info or spamming them. Professionals in the industry agree that 2-5 emails a month is a good number to set for email blasts. Too many and your customers will feel inundated. Too few and they may forget about you.

When sending coupons, remember to make them mobile optimized and include a numerical code or QR code (for QR enabled POS systems) so your customers can redeem the coupons in your establishment and not worry about leaving a print out at home.

Content is term that comes up more than once in this book. Content is any kind of media that is consumed by users of social media services. As Bill Gates once famously said, "Content is king." Content is a way that businesses interact with other social media users without pushing a sales pitch on them.

While people will expect some selling from your brand, a constant stream of coupons, offers, and enticements can become overwhelming and will lose effectiveness, not to mention generate ill will.

Experts agree that posted content should be a mix of value-added and promotional material that is mixed at a ratio of approxametly 80/20.

Experts recommend a balance of 80/20 added-value content to sales or promotional content meaning that 80% of your posts or touch points are non-sales oriented and roughly a maximum of 20% are.

To stand out from the competition, the content that you produce should have the have the following effect on other users. Content should:

Entertain

Inspire

Converse

Educate

Convince

The key item on that list is converse. Your content should start a conversation that generates customer engagement. Touch points are more effective when they involve participation and active, meaningful participation is an important method of attracting customers with your social media campaign.

No one business can be everything to everyone and not all content can be all of these things. A mix of a couple or several is great but don't be overly concerned if it is only one of these things. As your experience accumulates and your content generation prowess increase your content will become a better blend of the listed characteristics. The best way to learn about content generation is to check out the social media campaigns of big companies or brands that are doing it right. Check out some of your favorite brands and look at the content they are generating. Take notes with the list of content characteristics in mind. Don't be afraid to draw inspiration from what is currently out there.

A more detailed breakdown of which content is classified as what characteristic is included in the appendix of this book.

Quick Review

- ✓ A platform **is the technological environment in which users can interact with individual forms of social media.**

- ✓ **A** channel **is a direct method of communication within a platform such as a Facebook page or a Twitter account.**

- ✓ **A** user **is anyone who consumes social media content through an account with that platform.**

- ✓ The shift in online experience from static web pages to dynamic and user-generated content is known as the advent of Web 2.0.

- ✓ A social media campaign needs to have a purpose. Its goals should be outline using the S.M.A.R.T method which produces goals that are specific, measurable, achievable, realistic, and time-based.

- ✓ When launching a social media campaign, understand how it works in tandem with your brand's website

- ✓ A blend of both value-added and promotional content is best for brands. Experts recommend a ratio of 80/20, or 80% value-added 20% sales oriented.

Facebook

over a billion users and counting

Facebook describes itself as "a social utility that connects people with friends and others who work, study, and live around them". While this is certainly true, Facebook as a social utility is just the tip of the iceberg. Started in 2004, Facebook has become a go-to platform for many social media users and an embodiment of what has become the social media revolution. Facebook now has over a billion users[3] and while you won't have much of an effect marketing your pub or pizza shop to users in India this statistic demonstrates just how ubiquitous Facebook has become. This ubiquity also means that people will also trust Facebook as a source of information and as a presence in their lives.

From the standpoint of a user, Facebook lets those with a profile (Facebook's name for a user account) connect with other profiles and share their thoughts, pictures, and video. Users can "like" content or messages to demonstrate their approval and further share it with their own friends.

---

[3] The actual number is 1.19 billion monthly active users. 874 million of these are mobile users and of the 1.19B monthly users, 728 million are daily users. Source: The Next Web at thenextweb.com/facebook Jan 29 2014. Accessed May 15, 2015.

The tremendous ability of ideas and messages in the form of content to move from person to person is immediately apparent. The term "viral" is used to describe content that reaches a sort of critical mass in terms of how quickly it spreads and how ubiquitously it is represented across different social media platforms.

All of this is good news for you as a business owner but the best is yet to come. Unlike traditional online correspondence where faceless and sometimes nameless individuals interacted with one another, Facebook puts a name to the face so to speak. In addition to their name, Facebook users also provide large amounts of other personal information. The phenomenon of social media users becoming more comfortable with sharing personal information with various social media platforms is so pronounced that it has been given a name: Zuckerburg's Law. Named after Facebook co-founder Mark Zuckerburg, Zuckerburg's Law states that the rate at which people will be more comfortable sharing personal information with social media platforms will double annually. He hasn't been wrong yet.

This doesn't mean that as a business owner you have access to a database of email addresses and phone numbers. Facebook collects and aggregates all of this information into non-identifying meta-data. Meta-data is a term that is becoming more and more familiar with the advent and popularity of social media. Meta-data is essentially data about data. Information such as age, gender, or geographic location is parsed out of user profiles then assembled to examine trends and concentrations. This information is then used to break users into groups based on how their personal information stacks against meta-data about their habits, preferences, and characteristics. This information allows Facebook to make intuitive recommendations to users about which other users they may already know and to track progress internally. It is also the technology that makes targeted ads a reality. Targeted ads are the bread and butter of Google's AdWords service covered later in this book.

Getting Started with Facebook

As we discussed, a social media campaign should be a well thought out and planned enterprise. As with any marketing solutions effort there are a couple of questions you should be asking yourself:

How does Facebook fit into my overall marketing strategy?

How does Facebook fit into my social media strategy? Will Facebook be used in tandem with other social media platforms to achieve the same goals or will this be a stand-alone effort with specific goals?

Do I have the time and resources to commit to maintaining a Facebook presence?

It is important to understand and to plan the exact role that Facebook will play in marketing your business before launching a campaign that leverages the platform. To answer these questions, and to outline what you can get out of your Facebook page, let's take a look at some of the assets that Facebook offers businesses.

- Promotion **of products, services, events, and experiences**

- Creation **of excitement, interest through information and contests**

- Discussion **of popular topics, products and services directly with the people who will be consuming them; your potential customers**

- Group-**based interaction that includes numerous users who are like-minded (or have at least voluntarily joined a group)**

- Sharing **of media such as pictures and video to help convey your brand and values to your fans (and potential customers)**

Facebook is an excellent channel to utilize because it offers the ability to share a mix of information.

Putting it All Together

-1-

Identify the goals of your Facebook campaign. For many establishments Facebook is their go-to marketing channel because it is simply so popular and they have the ability

to express their content through a variety of mediums. Your goals should reflect your answers to the questions listed earlier in this chapter.

-2-

Create your Facebook page. The accounts many individuals have on Facebook are known by the platform as profiles. These are fine for personal use but the creation of a "page" on Facebook makes more sense for businesses. Pages for businesses have more freedom with fans; they're not limited to just 5,000 like personal profiles are. There are also a host of metrics that provide useful stats that can be helpful in determining the productivity of your Facebook channel.

Pages are managed by users with profiles, so in order to create a Facebook page, you will need to have an individual Facebook profile. It is important to note that one profile can manage multiple pages. Once a user "likes" a page, updates from the page will appear in their news feed.

Local Business or Place

Company, Organization or Institution

Brand or Product

Artist, Band or Public Figure

Entertainment

Cause or Community

Figure 1 The selection pane Facebook presents when starting a page. These options demonstrate what constitutes appropriate material for a page. Page creation can be done at www.facebook.com/pages/create

Once your page has been created it will be assigned a URL. This is a generated URL and is full of letters and numbers which makes it a little sloppy and difficult to convey easily to customers. The good news is, once your page received 25 "likes" you have the option of changing your page's URL.

-3-

Add content to your page. Upload pictures, links to video, and complete the biographical information for your business. Once this is complete, then you can share your new page with customers via your other social media channels and your established traditional marketing channels. It is a good idea to complete your page before sharing it to give your customers a cohesive, consistent, and complete experience.

Good content of course showcases your menu, your establishment, and your staff. Consider also sharing relevant articles, industry related material, and blog entries or other graphics that are native ads to take advantage of the 80/20 ratio, but skewed in your favor. Of course mention your other social media channels and provide links to your business' website. Facebook pages have the ability to schedule posts in advance so you can populate a calendar of posts in only one or two sittings.

Remember, this Facebook page is for your business. The content should be topical and reflect that fact. This is an opportunity for you to leverage the Facebook platform to grow and generate interest in your brand. Ultimately, what is appropriate for your establishment and your brand is your decision but it is safe to say that your business'

Facebook page is not the appropriate venue for videos of your cat.

-4-

Just about anything can be posted on Facebook so take advantage of that fact. Try to keep your posts engaging and use pictures and videos. Interactive types of content will always see better engagement than posts that are text only.

Quick Review

- ✓ **Facebook differentiates between accounts for individuals and businesses. A** profile **is an account for an individual while a** page **is an account for a business.** Pages **require an already established** profile **to administer and manage them.**

- ✓ **Facebook posts can consist of a variety of media that can be** scheduled **in advance. Facebook also offers a full suite of** analytics.

- ✓ **Posts that use** images or video **will see a much higher engagement rate on average than posts that are text only.**

Source: expandedramblings.com "Facebook User Activity Stats" Craig Smith
May 16, 2015

Country with the most active Facebook users: Canada

Daily active Facebook users in the US & Canada: 161 million

Percentage of all US senior citizens that use Facebook: 31%

Size of user data that Facebook stores: more than 300 petabytes

Percentage of active Facebook users that visit it multiole times a day: 56%

Note: A petabyte is 2^{50} bytes or roughly a thousand terabytes. A terabyte is a trillion (10^{12}) bytes.

Percentage of online adults that visit Facebook at least once a month

Number of minutes spent daily on Facebook per user

Percetage of monthly Facebook users that use it daily

Twitter

ideas shared at the speed of
6,000 tweets per second

Twitter is an online social networking service that allows users to send and read short (140 characters or less) messages called "tweets". The 140 character limit seems inhibitive but at a second glance it makes sense. At a rate of 6,000 tweets per second, a user's Twitter feed will be constantly updating. Of course not every user has that many tweets showing up on their stream but this number does put the scope of Twitter into perspective. This means that each individual tweet is highly transient and with the sheer volume of tweets, a long message would be completely lost. Throughout this chapter whenever a sample tweet is discussed the character count will also be listed in parenthesis. This is to demonstrate the fact that 140 characters, while a small cap, is still an extremely effective medium for the sharing of ideas.

Figure 2 A sample tweet. This example is an advertisement for Twitter's small business promotion services expressed as a tweet.

The above sample demonstrates the basic components of a tweet. In the upper left-hand corner you can see the user's account image. In this instance, the image is the icon for Twitter Small Biz. Personal accounts show a headshot (or other user selected image) and business accounts often show an identity graphic or other relevant branded image.

To the right of the user image is the name of the account that originated the tweet, and further right is the title of that account on twitter. All Twitter accounts start with the "@" symbol; its inclusion is the means by which the platform recognizes users. This line also include the date stamp for the tweet.

The text that reads "Interested in growing..." is the substance of the tweet. Personal tweets may read "Just landed at JFK. Grabbed a cab and on my way to the conference. I couldn't be more excited." (94 characters and yes that includes spaces). It may seem like the 140 character limit is over-emphasized here or harped upon a bit but the length (and therefore transience) is a defining characteristic of a tweet.

Below the content of the tweet is a user-provided image, below that is a series of action buttons. From left to right they read "reply", "retweet", "favorite", "follow", and "more options" with a record of the number of retweets and favorites listed next to their respective icons. When a user "follows" another user, that user's tweets appear on the followers' feed. "Retweeting" is the act of sharing another users' tweet to your own list of followers. A tweet that has been retweeted leads with the letters "RT". The act of retweeting is a powerful component of the Twitter platform, allowing different users to gain access to groups of people they would normally never interact with and thusly spread their sphere of influence. Marking a tweet as "favorite" preserves it to be looked at again later.

Another important component of the Twitter platform is the hashtag. A hashtag (written as #) acts as a categorization tag for a tweet meaning that many different tweets with the same topic (denoted by the text immediately following the hashtag) will show up in a search for that hashtag.

- #growyourbusiness

- #buildingsmallbusiness

- #getmoreears

An important note regarding the text of hashtags; the content of a "hashtag" has been determined to be commercial speech when published by a company. Defamation, false advertising, trademark infringement, unfair competition and false association are all legal trademark concepts that have been applied to the realm of hashtags. To date, there have been no lawsuits but cease and desist orders have been issued and there is little doubt that anyone wants to blaze the hashtag litigation trail.

So what is the value of Twitter for a business? Twitter serves a few very specific purposes.

- Establishment of credentials as leaders in the industry.

- Additional touch point for customers. Touch points are a two-way interaction where you hear the customers' needs and the customer hears your offerings. Generally speaking, the more touch points an organization has the higher their chances are of converting prospects into customers.

- Monitoring of the Twitter streams of competitors and seeing what their customers are saying about the quality of service and product offerings.

- Promotion of products, services, and events.

While the goal of Twitter is to accumulate followers, it is not to follow everyone. The more people that follow you, the higher the chances that your tweets will be retweeted and the larger your brand influence will grow. Following industry leaders or competitors can provide you with a steady stream of information, much of it actionable, following every @username that presents itself will inevitably crowd your Twitter stream and waste your time. Users that tweet about your personal interests should be followed with your own personal account. A business account is designed for just that: business. Allowing personal interests to cloud your business' Twitter account will ultimately make your presence more difficult to monitor as well as stunting your ability to measure your ROI.

That being said, the fast-moving quality of Twitter is a very effective way to maintain an eye on new developments within the industry. First and foremost this includes new products and services released by competitors. Knowing what to expect from the competition is a critical element in the process to produce a response. In the context of this publication we are discussing the bar and restaurant business so competitors are not limited solely to other establishments. Grocery stores, recipe sharing sites, and fast food restaurants all pose a threat to market share in addition to being goldmines for marketing ideas and new menu items. Non-direct competitors are also valuable sources of information.

Let's say that you own a burger shop in Philadelphia. @CaliBurgers posts a promotion for their new guacamole and fried onion burger that is gaining traction and generating discussion. If you're an owner trying to revitalize your menu on the East Coast, a West Coast offering called the California Burger could entice new customers and tantalize regulars.

This is a simple example but the point is that through the exploration of the industry new options are uncovered and become available. This exploration is made possible by the presence of social media and a wealth of ideas awaits anyone willing to take the time to look for them. Ultimately, you know your own customers and you know your brand. A level head coupled with a clear brand direction and concrete goals are all essential to a successful social media marketing campaign, whether on Twitter or on other social media platforms.

What happens if your business' Twitter account is used solely for promotion? People will lose interest. While followers will tolerate – and even expect – a certain level of promotion from following a business on Twitter a constant stream of contests, new products, and new services will tire even the most die-hard fan. If you are generating a consistent stream of promotion only tweets that's okay as long as they're spread out. A great way to break up the promotional barrage is to include "Top 10" and other informative style "native ads" to your tweet lineup. Remember the 80/20 ratio of value-added content to promotional or sales based posts (in this case tweets).

Just about everyone has an account with some social media service and a lot of people have accounts with more than one. Undoubtedly you have seen a "The top five ways to burn five pounds in 30 days" or a "Ten most brutal hits in the NFL" posts. What you may not realize is that these are less than altruistic posts. Many are in fact native ads or advertisements that have been written to look like anything but. To take an example that we have already been working with let's use the California Burger.

A great way to introduce a menu item that uses guacamole would be a "Five surprisingly healthy options at your local burger joint" article or blog post (we'll cover blogs later in this publication). This list would, among other things, extol the virtues of avocados and all the health benefits they can bring. It is common knowledge that avocados have health benefits but the presentation implies credibility and presents a fresh spin on information customers may already know. This list could be presented in conjunction with the launch of the California burger on the menu and the more channels that link to it, the higher your potential exposure.

Native ads also summarize or repurpose legitimate news or scientific findings. Through the camouflaging of information that supports your business it is possible to offer tweets that break up the stream of promotional dialogue with information that is valuable to both the customer and your business.

Twitter in Action

It is important to have followers on Twitter, but it is also important to follow. Many users will follow another user that follows them as a courtesy. While this is true that is generally considered a courtesy to follow someone who follows you, Twitter has imposed a limit on the number of users anyone can follow in an effort to prevent spamming. The limit draws a correlation between the users you follow and the users that follow you that ends up looking like a 1:1 relationship around 2,000 users followed. If at this point you don't also have 2,000 followers you will be capped in regards to the number of users you can follow.

When promoting your business on Twitter there are several important guidelines to remember. The first is that while many of your followers may be genuinely interested in keeping current with your business you are

While it is important to maintain a steady stream of tweets throughout a week, too many tweets will annoy followers. Stick to tweeting about relevant and value-enhancing topics.

competing with the huge number of tweets that are coming in on their stream. What this means to you is that in order to keep your business (and all of the great things that it offers) in the forefront of your customers' consciousness tweeting regularly is important. The more often you tweet, the better your chances of being seen by your followers. There is a limit however, no one wants to be thought of as a nuisance or spammer.

It is important to commit to a couple or even several tweets per day, especially during high traffic times. High traffic times would be the time of day when your customers would be checking their phones. Coincidentally, many of these times are designated as mealtimes so there is the added benefit of "follower participation". In the same sense that people who go to the grocery store hungry are in a "buying mindset", followers who are eating will be receptive to food-related content.

High-impact meal times vary from establishment to establishment. If you serve breakfast, keeping followers informed about options that are better than cereal and oatmeal is a good way to keep your establishment on customer's minds. Lunchtime is a critical time during the day to reach out to customers via social media. When followers are checking their phones for social media updates or catching up with friends putting your business on their minds is critical. If a group of coworkers is deciding where to meet for drinks after work and one of them has a coupon or knows about a happy hour promotion this can have an effect on the decision of the group as a whole.

Similarly, couples who contact one another on their lunch hour may be making dinner plans and a coupon or promotion for Twitter followers can tip the scales in a date night decision. Using Twitter as a marketing channel is about more than securing business for lunch – traffic that can also be impacted by Twitter – but generating interest for business later in the evening as well. Ideas for promotions include new and adventurous cocktails, half-priced appetizers for large parties, or dinner deals for two.

This leads us into another crucial aspect of generating interest through Twitter; making the experience special. Customer attention is a valuable resource and in marketing circles should be valued like gold. We have already discussed the fractured nature of the social media market and though it may sound daunting it is important to remember that not only are there thousands of competitors for attention on Twitter alone, but Twitter itself is competing for attention from other social media services as well. While at face value this may seem like a point against Twitter, the service is in fact an enabling force in the sense that even though the massive amount of information is seen as a continuous stream, its individual units are presented in easy-to-digest parcels that are highly transient. A business that wants to persuade its followers to become customers (or repeat customers, the best kind of customers) must provide value to followers and, to take that a step further, actionable or useful value is even better.

In practice, this is a very easy concept to implement. Coupon codes, code words for reduced price drinks and appetizers, or "on the spot" deals are all great ways to generate business for your establishment. In this context when we say "on the spot" we mean something like "Be here on Thursday the 10th between 7 and 9 to get half-priced apps!" This type of promotion would be applicable to all patrons between the designated hours but a tweet can reach infinitely more people than a sandwich board on the street (which is still an effective driver of passing foot traffic, don't pack up the sandwich board).

All of these Twitter marketing concepts are fantastic for followers and customers but they also provide your business with a key benefit (aside from interest, traffic, and customers). As we have already discussed, measuring ROI or the return on investment of a social media marketing campaign is an important business function. Using Twitter, a business can tweet a promotion such as "For this week only use the code "quesoplease" to get a free order of Queso Fries with any order" (95 characters). That's a cool deal for a customer but what it does for your ROI tracking is differentiates walk-ins from Twitter followers. If a customer uses the code "quesoplease" they could only have heard about it as a Twitter follower or as a friend of someone who is a Twitter follower. If you record the number of checks that used the code "quesoplease" you would have a rough idea of your return on investment for that tweet in particular.

Coupon or promotion tracking is an effective, if rudimentary method of measuring Twitter effectiveness. Technology can take a tally sheet out of the equation, sophisticated and modern POS (point of sales) systems can track coupon use through unique alphanumeric codes, bar codes, and QR codes (the square barcodes based on fractals). These are phenomenal tools at a business' disposal. Coupon use isn't only tracked but reports over time can show trends in the effectiveness of specific promotions and can really narrow down the effective times of day that a bar or restaurant can use to promote their business. The best decision is an informed one and with data on your side of the table the number of logical decisions can outweigh guesses and gambles.

If you have been in the dining game for any amount of time, you know how to be persuasive. It is important to let your personality shine through your tweets. This is *social* media after all. Your customers spend all day at work; the last thing they need now is another memo. This methodology is largely demographic specific however; you are the only one that understands your customer base. An informal, trendy tone may work for one establishment where a small town, local voice may be appropriate for another. Above all, remember that your business' Twitter account should not be used like your personal account. It may not be appropriate to bring up sensitive topics or inflammatory issues. Ultimately the content of your tweets is your decision; no one knows your customers like you do. Be aware though, on more than one occasion companies on social media have had to make very public apologies for PR accidents ranging from slip-ups to all out disasters.

A theme that we are always touching on is the time-sensitive capacity of Twitter and while this may seem a detriment it is also an asset that can be leveraged. Let's say for example that you have a surplus of asparagus on hand. A quick tweet that advertises something to the effect of "Halibut & grilled asparagus, asparagus & hollandaise, grilled asparagus & seasonal veggies. We have too much, half-price for u tonight only." (139 characters) can stimulate traffic and unload extra inventory. The same idea can be applied to slow weeknights. Let's say that an evening is going particularly slow. A quick tweet "Show this Tweet and get a FREE pint from 6-8 P.M. Tonight only!" (64 characters) can salvage a slow night and bring in otherwise lost business.

All of these examples have been Twitter specific and have been intended to get your creative juices flowing. Many of these tips are applicable to many social media platforms however. Right now you should be asking yourself "How can I tailor these examples to fit my business, my customers, and my brand?" Only you know the way to connect to your customers and the direction that your brand is headed but remember some critical advice concerning brands and their social media presence.

Social media platforms are many things to many companies but they are always funnels. Services like Twitter and Facebook act as user funnels to send users to your brand website and other social media services. This is an interesting concept because every aspect of a brand's presence should reflect the funnel and as we have already discussed the brand's presence should be a uniform and unanimous voice across all the platforms it inhabits. Cross-promotion is more than tweeting "Like us on Facebook" however, cross-promotion includes every incarnation of the brand from brick and mortar to Twitter and LinkedIn. A decal on your bar's window or a line on your restaurant's receipt that reads "Follow us on Twitter" is also a great way to get the most out of your social media campaign.

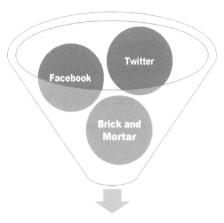

Unified Brand Perception

Overall, the concept of investing time and resources into a marketing medium that has only a chance of even being seen by the customer seems like bad business. Consider the following characteristics of the Twitter user base and Twitter's trending nature to see why Twitter is a good social media investment. First, those who have influence on Twitter are trendsetters. Trendsetters have a massive impact on the day to day decisions that those who follow them make. The more people a business can reach on Twitter, the higher your chances of reaching someone who is a trendsetter within their group.

Interaction on Twitter can be classified in four groups.

Tweets

Tweets are the 140 character messages we have already discussed. Tweets are sent to all of your followers and will appear in their Twitter stream. This is the method used to put out info, updates, promotions, and coupons. Tweets make up the bulk of interaction on Twitter and this is what your followers and customers will expect to see from your Twitter account.

Retweets

A retweet is a tweet that you have found by another user that you think your followers would enjoy or find informative. When a tweet is retweeted it includes the letters RT and the original user's name (@username). While the retweet function can have some utility for businesses, ideally it is your followers that will be using the retweet function to spread your tweets to their circle of friends.

A great tweet to retweet on the business side of the equation would be something a customer says positively about your establishment, or that they're having a great time there. Here is where the line between the customer's experience and their interaction with your business blurs. Let's say it's a couple's anniversary. They're having a great time and your bar manager has expressed his congratulations and thanked them for selecting your establishment to celebrate their special day. If they tweet that they're having a blast at your establishment then that is certainly worth retweeting to all of your followers. There is only one problem with this logic: time. Because tweets come and go so quickly it is easy for an individual tweet to get lost in the stream. Not all businesses want or can afford a full-time social media manager and even he or she may let something like that slip through the cracks.

The bottom line with retweets comes down to your particular business. You know what time you have to devote to a focused social media campaign and what you want to achieve with your campaign. Sometimes small (or in this case miniscule) opportunities slipping by is okay to preserve the big picture.

The Public Reply

A public reply is like a retweet but the original message is not preserved. This feature of Twitter is almost similar to a chat or message board in the sense that the reply is visible to other users. This is a great feature for all users of social media, personal and business alike, and it falls neatly into the dialogue aspect of marketing via social media. This allows users and followers within the Twitter channel to respond directly to a business' presence and vice versa.

Here the possibilities are endless. Let's say you have just tweeted "4-6 tonight half-priced pizza at the bar" (40 characters). A concerned customer can post a public reply with the question "I have a friend with a food allergy. Do you offer gluten free pizza?" (69 characters). To which you respond "The Corner Pub offers an extensive and delicious gluten free menu, please notify your server of any food allergies in your party. See u soon" (140 characters).

This exchange has put a concerned patron's worries at rest (assuming your establishment really does have a gluten free menu), encouraged them to visit your establishment, and reminded others that your establishment is sensitive to the needs of customers with food allergies. The first question that comes up with this example is "Why doesn't the customer just call us?" It's a good question. Out of Twitter's reported 302 million monthly active users, 80% access the platform from their mobile devices[4]. So it stands to reason that if these people are looking at Twitter on their phones they could just call and get an instant answer right? Kind of.

It is becoming increasingly common knowledge that millennials (defined as people reaching adulthood around the year 2000) are not interested in using their phones to make calls. A Wall Street Journal article from 2013 found

---

[4] Source: Twitter About https://about.twitter.com/company accessed May 14, 2015

that many millennials thought of talking on the phone to be an "interruption". If Twitter provides a barrier-free avenue for finding the information they want to know, your customers are going to use it.

Making reservations too is becoming done more and more commonly without a phone call. Many large restaurants are investing in web-based programs that allow customers to make reservations online. These programs alert hosting staff and automatically send a confirmation email to guests that outlines their reservation. Programs like this can prove to be logistical nightmares for businesses but guests love the convenience. It has been suggested that Twitter could act as a proxy for such programs and that guests could request reserved seating via Twitter. The next and final class of Twitter interaction would be best suited for this type of communication and we'll take a look at why.

Direct Messages

Direct messages can only be exchanged between two users who are following one another. They can only be seen by the sender and the recipient and are not public. Direct messages have little value for social media marketing campaigns in the broadcasting sense. They do have value in the interaction between a single customer and your business. Say a customer has a complaint on Twitter. Not all complaints are bad. Complaints offer you an opportunity to retain business and customers (namely repeat customers, the best kind) and address operations or products that may have issues. It is far better to have a customer complain about his or her experience and be receptive to amends than to stay silent and never patronize your establishment again. The ones that walk away quietly are the most potentially damaging to a business because they will use friends and relatives as an outlet for their frustration with your brand, two groups of people their opinion may have influence with.

So a customer complains on Twitter. This is not ideal, because usually businesses want to keep complaints quiet and address them on a case-by-case basis, but with the rapidly evolving and dialogue based environment of social media that is a scarce luxury. Depending on the nature of the complaint it may be appropriate to respond with a public reply. A public reply could address a protocol or operation that had been a source of complaints over time such as "We listened to you! Our downtown location now has improved lighting! Thanks for all your feedback, stop in to see how we're celebrating." (137 characters). If that's an appropriate avenue then great, you've told your customers you listen, you've addressed a concern, and promoted your business. If the tweet containing the complaint is very negative and the customer is a follower the direct message may be a better option to attempt to resolve the matter. Not all matters can be resolved however; this is an unfortunate fact of business.

Not all direct messages have to be under such circumstances. Thanking a well-known and frequent patron via direct message can solidify a business relationship and show your gratitude for the repeat business.

Figure 3 An example of a public response from a company with a fantastic Twitter PR team. @OctoberJones is a popular UK blogger who used wit to convey a complaint. Sainsbury's replied in kind with an effective response.

The response shown in the figure above is an example of a public response. This example illustrates exactly how a company can turn a complaint upside down using Twitter as a marketing channel.

Putting it All Together

Taking everything we've gone over so far regarding Twitter, let's compile that info and look at exactly what should be done for a successful social media campaign.

Identify the goals of your presence on Twitter. Tracking competitors, driving traffic with promotions and coupons, and real-time contact with customers are a few examples. Keep your goals in mind when executing the campaign. It is also important to prioritize your goals. If a circumstance arises where you will not have the time or the resources to dedicate to the management of a Twitter account it will be helpful to know which features of the platform you'll focus on and which you'll step away from.

For instance, if your coupon tracking is showing low coupon usage from Twitter and you have less time to commit to that channel of your marketing campaign, sending fewer coupons makes sense, but closing the account or pulling out of Twitter all together doesn't. The service may still be used to track competitors.

2

Create a Twitter account using your business name, for example @cornerpub. Accounts are free and easy to set up. Your Twitter user name is capped at 15 characters

and will appear on your profile along with your business name i.e. "Sadie's Corner Pub is @cornerpub". The newest incarnation of Twitter is the best yet for businesses with new profile layouts, new profile picture options and the ability to "pin" a tweet. Tweets that have been "pinned" will show up for visitors that check out your profile, giving you the option to keep a particular Tweet around and displayed prominently. Pinned tweets can be changed at your leisure. Don't forget to write a bio for your business (max 160 characters) to describe yourself to your customers and to the world.

Figure 4 The landing page for Twitter account creation at twitter.com/signup.

Lay the foundation. Twitter will recommend users for you to follow. Follow competitors and others in the industry. Look at who's following you as well. Kick-off your new account with a tweet like this:

"Hello Twitter! The best spot for wings in Sacramento is here! Stay tuned for updates, promotions, and freebies." (111 characters).

This first message isn't as important as many of your subsequent messages will be; your customers will probably never see this tweet. With that out of the way, explore Twitter, read FAQs, and check out some of the platform's features. Twitter itself has a variety of learning tools available for businesses on Twitter to grow their presence.

Remember, this is a business account and should be reserved for business purposes. Unless you run a politically themed bar, there is little apparent reason for your business to follow @WhiteHouse.

Get the word out. Mention your Twitter account across other social media channels, insert the Twitter logo on your menus, bills, and in the front window. Alternatively, a quick "Follow us on Twitter for updates, promotions & freebies @cornerpub" on menus and promotional material is just as effective as using the Twitter logo.

5

Being able to commit to a steady stream of tweets can be hard and tracking your tweets can be harder. Fortunately there are solutions, the most popular of which is a program called TweetDeck. TweetDeck is a free interface that allows multiple Twitter accounts to be maintained by multiple people. This feature is great for small businesses that have a team of staff sharing the social media load.

TweetDeck also allows the queuing, searching, and tracking of tweets and trends. Trying to boost a particular hashtag? TweetDeck provides trendspotting and trending analytics to assist. TweetDeck is worth a look even if the only feature you use is the tweet scheduling function (which can be very handy indeed.

Quick Review

- ✓ **A** tweet **is a short message that makes up the bulk of interaction on Twitter.** Tweets **are 140 characters or less, spaces included.**

- ✓ **User accounts on Twitter always begin with the "@" symbol.**

- ✓ **When a Twitter account is** followed **the tweets originating from that account will show up on the feeds of all followers. Followers are users that have subscribed to tweets from a specific account.**

- ✓ **A** hashtag **(#) acts as a tag for a tweet that groups with tweets about the same topic. The content of a** hashtag **is considered commercial speech. Don't infringe on copyrights or trademarks when writing hashtags.**

- ✓ Native ads **are advertisements that camouflage promotional material as casual or informative content.**

Percentage of active users that log on to Twiter more than once a day

Average number of followers per Twitter user

Daily active Twitter users: 100 million

Number of Twitter accounts that have ever sent a tweet: 550 million

Average time per month spent by users on Twitter: 170 minutes

Note: A quintillion is written as 1 followed by 18 zeros.

Total number of accounts that Twitter can handle: 18 quintillion

Percentage of world leaders that use Twitter: 80%

Top world leader on Twitter: US President Donald Trump

Instagram

300 million users means a lot of photos

Instagram is a social networking service centered on photo- and video-sharing. Content uploaded to Instagram can then be shared to other social networking platforms such as Facebook, Twitter, Tumblr, and Flickr. The first two on that list we have already covered, and the second two are featured later in this book. Instagram has gained very quickly in popularity and its success exploded in the later months of 2013. Some basic statistics about Instagram should tell you if it is the right social media tool for you. While use of Instagram seems to be split evenly between iOS and Android users, nearly 90% of Instagram's users are under the age of 35 and the gender use skews to nearly 70% female in the United States[5].

So if your target demographic doesn't fall inside this range, Instagram may not be your first choice for a social media marketing channel. That being said, thinking of a social media marketing campaign as a funnel, Instagram integrates with many other popular social media platforms and the ability to share straight to other accounts could

---

[5] Source: By the Numbers: 130+ Interesting Instagram Statistics Craig Smith May 23 2015 accessed May 23 2015 www.expandedramblings.com

prove to be a time saver. Let's look at some of the features of Instagram.

Photos shared on Instagram are confined to a distinctive square shape, different from the standard smart device aspect ratio of 4:3. This is especially significant because so far, Instagram is a mobile only platform. Uploaded photos can be assigned tags led by hashtags that denote a particular image as belonging to a specific community, or more commonly communities. It is a common practice by users of Instagram to tag their photos with numerous tags to increase the circulation and exposure of their content and therefore the number of "likes".

Another characteristic feature of Instagram is the ability of users to apply photographic filters to uploaded images along with modifications to other picture attributes such as contrast and saturation. This has given rise to the tag #nofilter, a tag assigned to photos that demonstrate a photographer's prowess and as such have been unmodified by an Instagram filter.

Figure 5 This popular image found on Wikimedia demonstrates each of the Instagram filters. Filters are more relevant for personal rather than business use of Instagram however employing filters can integrate businesses into the Instagram sub-culture in a more organic way.

The explore tab feature of Instagram allows users to search tags and recommends photos that they may be interested in based on their profile, connections and searches. Because the explore tab's recommendations are tailored to each individual user, no two users will see the exact same explore recommendations. Another component of the explore recommendation formula is geographic location. When photos are uploaded a geographic latitude and longitude may also be associated with the image file and each year Instagram ranks the top ten locales where pictures have been taken.

Instagram users can also upload videos, though the length is capped at 15 seconds. This feature has been seen by many as an attempt by Facebook (the current owner of Instagram) to compete with Twitter's Vine video-sharing application. Vine works in a manner similar to Twitter's "microblogging" service where videos up to six seconds can be posted, "revined" (read retweeted), and shared to Facebook and Twitter.

Instagram in Action

Instagram is a social media platform that revolves around smart devices. Capturing the interest of potential customers while they are on the go gives social media marketers more touch points which mean more opportunities to engage. At face value, Instagram doesn't seem like a great platform for businesses to interact with customers. On the contrary, Instagram can provide a highly engaging and participatory environment where businesses can produce meaningful and constant dialogue with users.

57% of Instagram users are checking their accounts daily[6], spending an average of 257 minutes (over four hours) a month actively using the service[7]. This is valuable time to capture. Even if Instagram followers don't become customers because of the interaction on Instagram, they can be funneled into following or liking your establishment on other marketing channels, increasing the number or touch points and exposure.

A variety of photos will always be better than just photos of food or drinks. Include Instagram posts of engaged staff or happy customers. Your establishment has great atmosphere, show it off and remind customers of the good time they're missing.

Just like all other forms of social media, Instagram requires regular updates. This channel is perhaps not as demanding as Twitter, which requires frequent updates, but due to the highly invested nature of users success on Instagram requires a complete profile and frequent posts. Since your posts will be pictures and not sentences it is

---

[6] Source: Pew Study Social Media Update 2013
[7] Source: L2 Intelligence Report Instagram 2014

important to grab the right pictures to convey your brand and to achieve your social media campaign goals. What should you include in Instagram photos? Take a look at the following examples and think about how they relate to your business and its customers.

You have spent a lot of time and money getting the environment and atmosphere of you bar or restaurant just so. A photo of a happy crowd enjoying your establishment is a great Instagram post. Engaged customers or staff also make great subjects for photos on Instagram. Pictures of promo flyers or banners to advertise are good candidates and these posts can increase the impact that promotional campaigns can have. DJ's, musical guests, guest bartenders, exciting new cocktails and new dishes are all also great photos to post.

Tagging these photos with the name of your establishment and the name of the event (if applicable) is a must in these examples. This is critical because even if people aren't searching for your establishment your guests will be taking pictures of themselves in your establishment. They will (hopefully) be tagging their photos with your establishment's name. It is a good idea to have the name of your establishment in a lot of visible areas. This way, even if photos aren't tagged, it will still be possible for people viewing them to identify the establishment.

Photos of just the food, drinks, and dining area can quickly bore followers. Consider using Instagram to introduce users to staff members, take "candid" shots of the kitchen with staff working (I use candid in quotes because shots like that are best staged), and photos of staff members helping out in the community. Is one of your employees in a band? Is there a popular landmark or scenic view nearby? Have any celebrities (local, national, or otherwise) eaten at your establishment? These are all things to share with Instagram followers as long as they fit your brand's image.

Your Instagram channel, as well as the rest of your social media channels, can be more than just photo galleries of you food and staff. Tell your brand's story in a creative way. The competition is fierce for creativity in social media, and if you can stand out, that alone will earn you some followers. You've stuck it out this long in the business, share with your followers (and the world) why you have a passion for the kind of food and drink that makes your customers come back for more.

Only using hashtags that include the name of your establishment is self-limiting. Think about the tags people may be searching or that people may be using in tags of photos taken in your bar or restaurant. A good way to find these tags is simply to search the name of your establishment with some regularity. For example, if a search yields a picture of three women enjoying drinks at the bar with the hashtag #girlsnightout, then that hashtag could be applied to ladies' night specials or other photos you upload. Similarly, an establishment in Portland could tag a photo #Portlandnightlife, #greatdininginportland, or any combination you can think of. Lines from popular songs about parties are excellent choices as well; many users will be tagging their photos #allnightlong or #shotshotshot and having your establishment in those search results will generate touch points and exposure. This last piece of advice is based on a judgement call however. You know your brand and your customers and it is up to you to determine which tags will be appropriate for your audience, customer base, and followers.

Tagging your photos with as many tags as possible will get you the most followers possible right? Maybe, but it's not a great idea. No one can be everything to everyone and tagging your posts with a massive amount of tags is considered poor social media etiquette. People will see that your tag-heavy pictures are an attempt to spam the system and it will turn them off to your photos and possibly your brand. It is better to be selective with your tags and select only those that are most relevant.

Photo booth #picstitch #love #TagsForLikes #TFLers #tweegram #photooftheday #20likes #amazing #followme #follow4follow #like4like #look #instalike #igers #picoftheday #food #instadaily #instafollow #like #girl #iphoneonly #instagood #bestoftheday #instacool #instago #all_shots #follow #webstagram #colorful #style #swag #fun #instagramers #TagsForLikes #food #smile #pretty #followme #nature #lol #dog #hair #onedirection #sunset #swag #throwbackthursday #instagood #beach #statigram #friends #hot #funny #blue #life #art #instahub #photo #cool #pink #bestoftheday #clouds #amazing #TagsForLikes #like #all_shots #textgram #family #instago #igaddict #awesome #girls #instagood #my #bored #baby #music #red #green #water #harrystyles #bestoftheday #black #party #white #yum #flower #2012 #night #instalove #niallhoran #jj_forum #guys #guy #boy #TagsForLikes #TFLers #boys #love #me #cute #handsome #picoftheday #photooftheday #instagood #fun #smile #dude #follow #followme #swag #sexy #hot #cool #kik #igers #instagramers #eyes #friend #friends #fun #TagsForLikes #funny #love #instagood #igers #friendship #party #chill #happy #cute #photooftheday #live #forever #smile #bff #bf #gf #best #bestfriend #lovethem #bestfriends #goodfriends #besties #awesome #memories #goodtimes #goodtime

Figure 6 Too many tags on a photo. Having too many tags is seen as poor social media etiquette and can negatively impact your brand's perception on channels such as Twitter and Instagram.

Putting it All Together

-1-

Just like all of your social media channels, before stepping up to the plate, know your goals and how Instagram will help you get there. Instagram is about photos. It is a good idea to have a sense of what direction you want to head in with your photos, your brand, and your customers. Telling your brand's story visually is very trendy right now

and Instagram users currently represent the trend-setting segment of the population.

-2-

Create an Instagram profile. Pick a name that clearly identifies your business or, if the name you want is already taken, select one that is a best fit. Complete your profile with your logo, bio, and of course a link to your website.

-3-

Connect your account to Facebook. Facebook owns Instagram, so the connection between the two accounts will be seamless. If you know you'll be uploading tons of pictures consider creating an Instagram tab on your Facebook page that showcases all of your Instagram content. You worked hard to produce all of those photos, makes sure everyone gets to see them. When deciding which photos to upload to Instagram consider selecting exclusive content. Much in the same way we can create artificial variety by taking different shots of the same subject, so too can we create artificial exclusivity. Take a single photoshoot, or one round of the employees with a camera that generates several dozen photos. Divide them up amongst your social media channels so no two have the same pictures. Offer coupons and promos for one channel only. This means that as people learn about different deals on different channels they will be encouraged to check out all of you channels.

-4-

When uploading photos to Instagram, don't forget hashtags. Some experts recommend between six and fifteen hashtags for Instagram uploads, but remember the picture of the wall of hashtags, many of which were reused? Don't let that be you. Focus on trending hashtags as well as generic hashtags. Trending hashtags could be a new brand of liquor that you (definitely not a coincidence) make a new cocktail with or a food related viral sensation (they're more common than you think). Cover your bases. In addition to tags that match your products and demographic, think about how you can break into searches that may not be directly about your establishment or product.

#Italianhomecooking

#pastaparadise

#spagetti&meatballs

#greatItalianrecipies

#familycomesfirst

#labellavita

#thegoodlife

#morewineplease

#passthegrappa

All of the above hashtags are Italian themed (in this instance we are the proprietor of an Italian family restaurant). Though they all have Italian flair they are not about restaurants per say. This method is designed to bring you followers that may not have been looking for your restaurant in the first place. Searching the hashtags you are thinking of will help you decide if they are right for your business. Of course, look at the hashtags your competitors are using too. If they're using a hashtag that is getting them into new circles, you should be there too.

Using brand specific hashtags is also a good idea. Using your establishment's name as a hashtag

(#GiulianisItalianSpot) on each of your Instagram posts will help people who are searching for your business on Instagram find you. Coming up with unique hashtags for contests or promos can also be an effective way to drive participation.

When running contests on Instagram remember a few key things. First, make sure you're giving away something that will entice and incentivize people. No one will want to participate in a contest that is giving away a useless prize. Second, never forget that this contest isn't just for you to give away money. A contest should benefit you and end up being worth the price of admission (the prize). When running a contest on Instagram the following would be a good template to use.

1. **Use all of your marketing channels (traditional and social media) to promote the contest, along with the entry rules.** *"Giuliani's Italian Spot is giving one lucky guest a $250 gift certificate to our restaurant.*

2. **The entry rules should advance your restaurant and your campaign.** *"To enter to win, follow us on*

Instagram (giulianisItalianspotNY), and post a picture of your last visit. Tag it #labellavitaNYcontest and don't forget to smile!"

3. **This contest gives you Instagram followers, pictures of people enjoying your establishment, and traffic inside your establishment.**

Contest results are displayed together, and the content can be displayed across other channels in your marketing campaign. Don't forget to monitor your hashtags like you would any other aspect of your social media marketing campaign.

-5-

Make your followers famous. As your following develops, look at some of the posts your fans are making. If they make sense with your demographic and your brand, repost them and give a shout out to the original user. *"Wanted to share this pic of our friend Angela's hydrangea bush. Great green thumb!"* **Maybe not hydrangea bush, but you get the idea.**

Liking and commenting on your follower's photos makes the exchange personal, but demonstrate tact when applying this method. It may not be appropriate to comment on family photos so sticking to pictures people have at your establishment or are relevant to your brand or business is a safe bet. Good news, people take a lot of pictures of themselves eating and drinking.

Instagram now allows you to embed photos within your website, blog, and other social media channels. This is a great way to show off the relevant posts your followers produce across your entire campaign. @mention your customers, celebrities, and other industry leaders in relevant photos as well. This means they will see the post and may repost or respond.

For a fantastic example of the Instagram customer engagement process check out coffee monolith Starbucks' Instagram page. Starbucks completely understands the Instagram platform (they're also killing it at just about every type of social media there is) and is leveraging it to the utmost.

-6-

Keep an eye on your posts. Social media is not a "set it and forget it" venture but rather a dynamic exchange between your brand and your customers. Respond to all comments on your posts. This means the good, the bad, and the ugly. Remember, not all customers can be saved. Offer words of encouragement and thanks to those that praise your brand and exercise patience, restraint, and professionalism with those that criticize it.

-7-

Once you have your presence on Instagram established, drive engagement with your posts through the most basic method possible: ask. Encourage your followers to post comments on your pictures and videos. Questions create conversations and asking your followers "what do you think?" about your posts can drive engagement and conversation. Don't limit these questions to your posts. Encourage your followers to talk about your business, your brand, or your food. "Hey, @billmith, what did you think of the grilled asparagus as a seasonal veggie? Tom in the kitchen hates asparagus." Engagement can also come from "fill in the blank" posts. A picture of a coffee bean that says "I should be served for the best taste" can get people talking about your new cold brew at your café.

Asking your followers to caption your photos can be effective as well. Post a picture of an employee being silly and ask your followers to caption it, or better yet, insert a speech bubble to encourage followers to engage with your photos. For a fantastic example of this method in action, check out GrubHub and their photo caption campaign.

Since this *is* social media, don't be afraid to crowdsource photos as well. Asking followers for their photos showing them enjoying your establishment is a great way to develop your Instagram profile.

Quick Review

- ✓ **Instagram is a** picture and video-sharing **social media platform. Like all social media marketing channels it requires frequent updating and maintenance.**

- ✓ **Instagram is a** mobile only **platform.**

- ✓ **Like tweets on Twitter, Instagram's photos are organized by** hashtags (#) **which denote pictures as belonging to a specific group or community.**

- ✓ **Use Instagram to** visually tell your brand's story.

- ✓ **Using a number of different** tags **will allow users and followers to find your pictures but be careful not to spam photos with too many tags. Use only tags that are relevant.**

- ✓ Hashtag contests **on Instagram can be used to grow your following and make your followers famous.**

Source: By the Numbers: 130+ Interesting Instagram Statistics Craig Smith
May 23 2015 accessed May 23 2015 www.expandedramblings.com

Estimated number of U.S. Instagram users (2015): 77.6 million

Estimated percentage of U.S. pop. that uses Instagram (2015): 27.6%

Estimated number of U.S. Instagram users by 2018: 106.2 million

70% of Instagram users are from outside of the U.S.

30% of U.S. teens consider Instagram the most important social network

Number of Instagram photos that have been shared

Most liked Instagram photo ever (look it up)

Percantage more likes that photos with faces recieved than without

Google

harnessing reliance on the most
popular "g" word

Google+

Google+ is the relatively new social media platform that exploded into the public's consciousness in 2012. The number of active users rose at an incredible rate, due in part, to the fact that every new Gmail account was automatically assigned a Google+ account as well. This doesn't mean that the Google+ landscape is a ghost town populated by shell accounts; Google+ uses some special features that set it apart from other social media services.

The business differentiated side of Google+ is called Google My Business and it allows businesses to build a business page (as different from a personal account, similar to a Facebook page vs. Facebook profile) that is focused on collaborating and networking with other businesses and engaging customers.

Google is developing an impressive suite of programs for their customers and they understand that putting all of their tools at users' fingertips is the way to secure loyalty. What this means for you is streamlined integration of Google products like insights, Google AdWords, Maps, and

Google Places. Google Places is covered later in this chapter and is a component of your total Google+ experience

---

Google AdWords is Google's popular PPC (pay per click) ad service. The service costs nothing unless visitors actually click on your ad; whether or not they turn into paying customers is up to you. The world of PPC advertising is complex and unique. Ads can be targeted to localities, certain timeframes, and are always targeted to users who are searching relevant terms.

Google Maps is Google's geographic mapping extension. It provides directions to addresses in real time, frequently updated street and satellite views, and helps Google's other services understand where your business is in relation to your customers.

Google

coffee shop in new york   🔍

Web   Images   Videos   Shopping   News   More ▾   Search tools

Freshly Brewed Coffee
Ad cafe.example-business.com
Always perfectly brewed coffee. The perfect way to start your day.

Start your morning with Only Fresh Coffee
www.onlyfreshcoffee.com/ ▾
Only Fresh Coffee has been family-owned and operated since 1986. We're dedicated to serving the freshest coffee, brewed from beans we roast ourselves. Drop by our friendly neighborhood store and enjoy a cup today.

Local Fresh Coffee
www.localfreshcoffee.com/ ▾

Figure 7 A search result showing a Google AdWords advertisement. The first result labeled as an Ad with the yellow icon is not an organic search result.

Google+ also uses a functionality known as circles. Circles are like groups on Facebook but content can be tweaked to fit a particular circle in the spirit of market segmenting. Content can be tailored to a specific circle which allows you to target different localities, age groups, and customers with ease.

Google Places

Google Places isn't a traditional social media platform in the way that Twitter or Instagram is, but it is a product of

what is considered Web 2.0 and a component of the Google stable of programs. Integrated as an element in your social media marketing campaign, Google Places can be an effective tool for funneling interest and traffic to your business. Additionally, the business review system that Google supports can drive conversion from interested browser to paying customer. Every second, Google process over 40,000 search queries which translates into over 3.5 billion searches per day. Worldwide that's 1.2 trillion searches per year[8]. Trillion with a "t".

People are conducting more searches than ever and those numbers are trending upwards. Relevant for our purposes is the number of searches that are conducted to learn local information. Digital data analytics company ComScore found that as much as 56% of mobile-based "on the go" searches had local intent[9] and that number could potentially be rising. That's great news for restaurants and bars, but only if your business is showing up in the results.

---

[8] Source: www.internetlivestats.com/google-search-statistics/ accessed May 15, 2015
[9] Source: Search Engine Land "Research: 56 Pct. Of "On The Go" Searches Have Local Intent" Greg Sterling May 6, 2014

The search engines of the past relied on keywords in queries that would be matched to content on web pages to connect searchers with what they were looking for. Today's search engines are much more advanced, engaged, and proficient at matching results to searches.

Google, in its race to become the go-to source for all information on the Internet, realized that allowing businesses to update or modify their own entries in Google's search results would stimulate more accurate entries and produce an enhanced user experience.

Figure 8 The well-known Google location marker.

Google Places is an interface for businesses to control how people searching on Google will see their business.

The platform has incrementally been getting more intuitive and helpful to both businesses and potential customers, but now the system is at its peak (for now, new innovation may be just around the corner).

Businesses that create an account with Google Places can customize many of the listed attributes that people searching for their establishment will see. New businesses may have to verify their location via postcard. In this instance a postcard is mailed to you with a code to input in your Google Places dashboard. Most established businesses will simply have to verify their business via a code received by phone. Verification is both simple and important. Google favorably ranks businesses that are verified over those that are not.

Once inside the Google Places interface with your business located you have the option of uploading photos, video, store hours and more to be shown with your entry in Google's search results. Below is a list of some of the features the Google Places platform.

- Menu options **can be uploaded, giving customers the option to preview your menu from their home computer or smart device.**

- Photos **can be uploaded. Photos should be of entrées, staff, the establishment itself or exciting cocktails. While the urge to recycle photos from one platform to another may be high, a good idea is only to recycle photos of the establishment's exterior. We'll discuss why in a second.**

- Video **can be uploaded, with a limit of five YouTube videos per account.**

- Operating hours **can be posted making a quick Google search a one-stop shop for what seems like the most common customer inquiry. Those of you in the restaurant business know what I'm talking about.**

- Payment options **can be posted to reassure them that you accept all major credit cards. Many establishments are also now accepting payment via digital financial services such as PayPal.**

- Coupons **can be posted with your Google Places result that customers can print out and bring to** your business. If you have a **QR code enabled POS,** there are some clever ways to circumvent having to print the coupon at all (a way to streamline the experience for your customers).

- Reviews **can be posted by customers. The effects of positive reviews should be self-explanatory, but if you're not convinced, one survey found that 90% of consumers' buying decisions are influenced by online reviews**[10]**. That means bad reviews too.**

- Analytics and insights **are available for your business such as where customers are coming from to patronize your business, what types of food they're searching for and more.**

All of these are fantastic assets for your business; let's look at how some of these tools can be leveraged to get the most out of Google Places.

Allowing customers to preview your menu is great. If you are vigilant with your social media campaign, your menu

---

[10] Source: Marketing Land "Survey: 90% of Customers Say Buying Decisions Are Influenced by Online Reviews" Amy Gesenhues April 9, 2013

is available on your website and can be viewed on your Facebook page. This also means keeping each channel's version of your menu updated as well. You work hard to build your menu and craft it to entice customers, make sure your customers can see the product of your work.

Photos and video are excellent additions to your Places entry. As you develop your profile and add more media content not only will you produce a higher impact search result, but you are also contributing to the enhancement of Google users' experience. Google will reward you with increased "authority" which is to say that your entry will rank favorably.

The urge to recycle photos across platforms can be high. This is an acceptable practice for photos of the exterior for your establishment. Consistency with the portrayal of your business' façade will help anchor customers who are interacting with your bar or restaurant across multiple channels. Like it or not, the front door to your eatery or bar is as much its face as a selfie is to you or I. Keeping that image consistent will give your customers "landmark recognition" and will help them associate your establishment with the other images they're seeing.

When it comes to photos of entrées, appetizers, and drinks high quantity and high quality are the name of the game. If a customer is on your Facebook page and sees a picture of the risotto from one angle, then searches your establishment the next day to see your business hours and a picture of the same risotto from a different angle is presented to her you are in effect branding your risotto. She is looking at The Corner Pub, keeps seeing your delicious risotto from different tantalizing angles, and keeps saying to herself "Wow, that risotto looks good" without getting bored with the same picture.

Different pictures of the same subject create artificial variety and what I call "entrée-level touch points". These touch points are exposure of your food to your customers and if all goes well, they may patronize your establishment because they

Photos taken from several different angles of the same subject create artificial variety. In effect, this method is "branding" your risotto, creating multiple touch points with customers centered on your entrées.

have become enamored with the food and they know your business is the place to get it. Don't be upset; you worked hard on delivering the total package of food, drink, and a fun atmosphere but a paying customer is a paying customer. Plus, if your risotto can't be beat, she may become the best kind of customer. At this point I don't even need to say "repeat".

Videos also make excellent additions to your Google Places entry. Videos, along with their suggested content, are discussed in the YouTube related chapter of this book. Suffice to say here though that Google's insistence that YouTube be the format of all featured videos is not a detriment but in fact a sigh of relief. Reliance on the largest online video-sharing network means stability and reliability for all parties involved.

Operating hours and payment options are basic, qualifying information about your business. Their inclusion in your places entry is so simple that it could only be the product of carelessness or laziness that they would be left out. Additionally, think of how the customer would see an error like that: "They have videos, photos, and their menu but there's no operating hours? Who does that?"

Google Places also allows you to post coupons for your customers. Initially, the thought was that customers could print them out at home and bring them to your establishment. While many people may still do this, it is a good idea to put a numeric code or even a QR code (if your business has a POS with a QR scanner) on the coupons so customers can show them while they're patronizing your business. This means there will be less accommodations for customers who left their coupons at home and increased accuracy with tracking your coupons' effectiveness.

The data analytics that Google Places offers is easily the biggest asset provided by the service. Information such as who's searching for you, how they're finding you, and where they're coming from to visit your establishment are all extremely beneficial statistics that can be used to make smarter business directions.

You know the kinds of people who make up your demographic, and you know who you market to. Knowing what kind of people are coming to your business is a great feedback tool to see just how effective you have been as well as determining if staying the course is the right move, or if adjustments are necessary.

Information regarding the ways people are finding your business is another feedback channel. This can help you identify opportunities and can provide evidence of productive marketing methods.

Putting it All Together

Now that we have covered how Google Places is an asset to your business, let's look at the steps needed to use this platform as a part of your social media campaign.

-1-

Identify the goal associated with modifying your Google Places entry. In this case, the search result is already there, you're picking the information that shows up for people searching your business so the goals here are based around building awareness, building your brand, and utilizing Google's analytics as a feedback program to make smarter decisions.

-2-

Verify your business via phone or postcard (if necessary). Verifying your business with Google is the first step in bringing your entry to the top of the search results. Upload your photos and video content. Multimedia is another component in the equation that determines which result will appear first. For ideas, search generically for your establishment such as "restaurants in Portland" and take a look at the top entry. That establishment has the top result for a reason. In the next several steps we'll cover how to boost your business' position within the results ranking.

-3-

From your Google Places account dashboard (the dashboard is the heads up landing page) you can select categories for your establishment. There is no reason not to use all five, in fact your competitor probably is. In addition to the obvious entry of bar or restaurant consider pub, tavern, Italian cuisine, pizza shop, nightlife, nightclub, first-class dining etc... The more categories you have, the higher your chances of getting paired with the variety of search terms that people will use. While it is true that Google (and other search engines) no longer rely strictly on keywords, taking advantage of such categories ensures that fewer searches will pass your business by.

-4-

Adding citations is a critical way to boost the rank of your entry. Here citations mean supporting authority on the existence of your business. This means, first and foremost ensuring that you have a business web page established. This will immediately improve the position of your entry in Google's search results. In addition, making sure that your business is listed in multiple online directories will improve the integrity of your citations and boost your results. There are a massive amount of online business directories, far too many to list here. Basic searches will yield results for the most popular.

Again, looking at the entries of competitors that are ranked first and searching their business will give you an idea of what it takes to bring your business to the number one slot what directories you should be placing your business in.

-5-

As your business is patronized, so too will it accumulate reviews. Earlier in the chapter we discussed how Google members can post reviews on business entries. A business with a lot of reviews will earn a higher rank in Google's results list. This process can take time and it is important not to attempt to subvert the system. As we will examine in the following section concerning Yelp! and similar services naturally building a collection of authentic and organic reviews is favorable to cheating your way to false reviews.

Google is not the only provider of a service like Places. Google competitor Yahoo! has a service called Yahoo! local that essentially provides the same experience for businesses but for a fee. Named Yahoo! Localworks, this service mirrors Google Places with established accounts having the opportunity to build a profile that features multimedia content, tracks stats from users, and shares reviews. Unlike Google's free platform, Yahoo! Localworks also guarantees placement in over 50 online business directories with modifications to your business profile pushed to each directory entry in real time to ensure accuracy and continuity.

Source: By the Numbers: 80+ Google Search Statistics Craig Smith May 23, 2015 www.expandedramblings.com

| Google Share of U.S. Search Market: 75.2% | Google Share of U.S. Mobile Search Market: 87.1% | Number of webpages indexed on Google: 50 billion |

Utah is the state that uses Google the most in the U.S.

% The number of Internet
rs that Google themselves

Average duration
of a visit to
Google+

Percentage of
small businesses
that use Google+

Google+'s share
of total online
social sharing

A Word about Yelp! And Similar Services

There are quite a few services out there that are purpose-built to let people talk about their exierences. And people love to talk about their experiences. Nothing gets more attention then bad reviews and a really bad review can circulate virally. Yelp! is a popular platform that crowd sources reviews from users all over the country and acts as a sort of public forum. What sets this apart from the other topics of this book is that participation on Yelp! is not optional or voluntary. Businesses cannot elect to be reviewed on Yelp! and have little recourse to fight negative publicity.

We've all seen a bad review from a dissatisfied customer. Some of these have merit such as "We ordered fries and were double billed. Management refused to refund the accidental billing." Others do not such as "The meatball sandwich was the worst I've had in my life" or "I wasn't allowed to use the patio because it was raining" (both are paraphrased actual reviews on Yelp!).

Reviews, even bad ones have value to a business. Poor reviews that point out issues are oppurtunities for you to improve your business. Positive reviews are obviously a great way to share the fruits of your labor and grow your base of dedicated customers. Knowing the impact that reviews have on customers' decsion making process good reviews are essential to drawing new customers to your business. Yelp! has given businesses a chance to respond to negative reviews. Accounts are free and the oppurtunity to respond to negative reviews is certainly an asset for businesses. This system allows contact under circumstances of the opposite nature as well. Many establishments on Yelp! will thank reviwers for their vist, their kind words, and invite them back.

When thanking a reviewer for sharing their positive experience the urge to promote your business may be present. It isn't recommended that thank you messages be anything more than a simple thank you. It isn't ideal for a business to be thought of as bribing reviewers or encouraging customers to leave positive reviews in exchange for discounts or deals.

When thanking a reviewer for their kind words, don't respond with coupons or discounts. Online reviews are normally seen to be without bias and the negative PR stemming from a scheme like that would outweigh any short-term gains.

Trust and fairness in reporting form the basis for crowd sourced reviews. Reviews, especially positive ones, are seen to be without bias. People who use review sites place trust in other reviwers and see manipulaton of the system as a violation of that trust. The potential storm of negatie PR coming from discovery of a scheme like that would certainly outweigh any short-term gains.

In circumstances where you would prefer your response seen by all, there is an option to post a pubic reply to a user's review. This is an opportunity to diffuse a negative review by putting a customer's concerns at ease while simultaneously demonstrating to other readers that you value customer input and that you are willing to listen to constructive suggestions.

Yelp! is by no means the only crowd sourced review website. Other popular cuisine related review sites include Eat24, OpenTable, Urbanspoon, Zagat, Gayot, GrubHub, and MenuPages. Each of these services has a differentiating factor; OpenTable acts like the Priceline of table reservations and GrubHub allows users to place online orders for eateries that are in network.

Each of these services increases your exposure with customers and gives you a wealth of reviews that you can quote on your Facebook page or share as a link via Twitter. While it can be scary knowing that bad reviews can spread like wildfire, remember that most people are fairly reasonable and understanding. If you are unfortunate enough to be hit with a wave of poor reviews, read them. Respond if possible or appropriate and learn from them before moving on.

Tumblr

making microblogging work for you

Tumblr is a social media platform that allows users to share different types of media in a short blog format; hence the name microblogging. If there is something on the Internet, rest assured there is a micro version of that same thing online as well.

True to the social media form, Tumblr allows users to follow the posts of others and discuss posts and topics as a community. Popular posts can be "reblogged" or shared again much the same way that tweets can be retweeted.

The Tumblr "About" page describes the site best: "Tumblr is so easy to use it's hard to explain. We made it really, really simple for people to make a blog and put whatever they want on it... Tumbler is 237 million different blogs, filled with literally whatever."

While conceptually Tumblr is a fantastic platform for people who love to create and consume content it is more content-oriented than platforms such as Facebook. Facebook as a service is about connecting people who

know each other and growing their networks. Tumblr on the other hand lets people discover and share their content with strangers. As a result, Tumblr has a much lower usage rate than social media sites such as Facebook, Twitter, and Instagram. Business Insider reports that the service probably has between 30-50 million active users; this statistic has been inferred from other information however as the company has not voluntarily released any numbers confirming or refuting this fact[11]. While all signs point to an upward trend since the release of this statistic, Tumblr is still trailing industry leaders in the size of its active user base.

Figure 10 Tumblr's logo, a stylized lower-case "t".

Here's another interesting statistic about Tumblr: The platform has much more lax regulations on what is considered prohibited content and as a result the service

---

[11] Source: www.businessinsider.com "The Truth About Tumblr: Its Numbers Are Significantly Worse Than You Think" Jay Yarow May 21, 2013

is home to a considerable amount of adult content. (NOTE: at press time, Tumblr has now banned adult content.) While this has little specific relevance to the topic of this book it should be noted for the proprietors of family restaurants approximately 10% of Tumblr domains are dedicated to content labelled NSFW (not safe for work)[12]. Users without adult content filters enabled will almost certainly come across pornography at some point in their digital travels on Tumblr.

Tumblr is a fantastic platform for a social media marketing channel because it blends different mediums of communication into one platform. The dashboard is the primary tool for Tumblr users. The dashboard includes a feed of posts from other users you follow where you can like, comment, and reblog posts as you see fit.

---

[12] Source: www.dailydot.com "Tumblr's massive porn stash—by the numbers" Kevin Collier May 20, 2013

The dashboard is also the tool through which content is uploaded. From the dashboard users can upload posts consisting of text, images, videos, and links to other blogs. Tumblr is a content consumption environment so the more content and the more varied the content, the better. Like many blogs, Tumblr also has an html editing function that allows you maximum creative control over the way your post will look.

Each post can be tagged to enable quick location and optimize searches. Tags are an integral part of social media categorization and an effective way to get found whether you are on Tumblr, Instagram, YouTube, or any tag-employing social media service. The dashboard also has a queue feature that allows users to schedule posts to be automatically published in the future.

For businesses attempting to leverage Tumblr, keep in mind its position as a creative outlet. Contests are a great way to engage followers and a picture contest would be an effective promotion but think about the multimedia side of Tumblr. Consider a recipe contest instead as a "virtual cook-off". Contests that allow fans to propose new dishes or cocktails for your establishment are also better suited to the Tumblr environment. Just like with Instagram, make your Tumbler followers famous by highlighting the winner of your competitions with your Tumbler posts.

Humor is a common theme on Tumblr and finding a way to make that work with your brand and demographic (I need to phrase it like that but come on, who doesn't like to laugh?) will build your following on Tumbler and increase your chances of viral status. Businesses can pay to have content put in front of customers through paid posts but views accumulated this way are not the same as achieving truly viral content.

If you are going to take the paid post route, consider the fact that though you got another set of eyeballs on your post you have to try much harder to get through to the viewer. In instances where the come across your content themselves they are much more likely to become engaged instead of waiting for your content to be over because they *have* to see it. Paid posts must be truly innovative and engaging to produce effective results that entice people despite themselves.

To capture the momentum of trends, monitor trending tags and use memes to ride the growing interest. Memes are usually a combination of pictures and text with a humorous message or result. Some companies have perfected using replaying animated GIFs as memes and are leveraging that content to build their brand recognition and perception.

The bottom line with producing Tumblr content is ensuring that it is creative, artistic, or funny enough to merit a reblog. Reblogs get you access to new groups of people and that's the fastest way to spread your influence on Tumblr. Look to businesses with a large following on Tumblr to see what works for them and imitate their content to carve out your own niche for your brand's Tumblr content.

Putting it All Together

-1-

Set goals for your presence on Tumblr. Set goals and have a plan before creating your Tumblr profile. Tumblr is a microblogging platform that supports diverse amounts of media. Know that you will have to use artistry, humor, and creativity to promote your brand on Tumblr.

-2-

Create a profile. Once your profile is created brand your page with your logo, cover photo and bio. Look at what other businesses who have large Tumblr following are doing and imitate their assets. Follow trendsetters and other Tumblr bloggers whose posts you can reblog to blend their content with yours to add value for your customers and followers.

-3-

Start posting content. Because Tumblr can support such a wide array of content the sky is the limit here. Remember to pull out all the stops to produce memorable and more importantly reblog-able content. Don't promote your content until you have a robust page but when you do get there use Tumblr's built in links to automatically post to Facebook and tweet when you submit a new post. Take advantage of the dashboard's queue feature to schedule posts and save time.

Use contests and humorous content to engage customers. Quizzes, contests, and polls are all easily linked from Tumblr posts. Dive into the discussion and make your followers famous by mentioning them and commenting on their content. If their content is especially helpful and in line with your brand, reblog it and maybe they'll return the favor.

Quick Review

- ✓ **Tumblr is a** microblogging **platform that allows users to upload a multitude of different content formats from the service's main point of interaction with users,** the dashboard.

- ✓ **Tumblr has a high degree of focus on** content consumption **and** humor.

- ✓ **Like all social media services, content that has varied types of media will see higher engagement than text-only posts.**

Number of Tumblr Posts: 99 billion	Number of Tumblr Posts: 113.6 million	Total Monthly Tumblr Visitors: 199.1 million

Top viral Tumblr blog of 2013 "Reasons My Son is Crying"

Average duration of Tumblr visit in minutes

Average number of times a Tumblr post is reblogged

Average number of times sponsored Tumblr posts are reblogged

Pinterest

pin, repin, repeat

Pinterest is a content sharing service that allows users to upload, save, and share images known as pins. Pins act like bookmarks that link back to the original content so the better content you produce the more traffic you'll generate. The name and concept is derived from the idea that a user's Pinterest page is like a virtual pin board, allowing them to pin up and take down images as they see fit. Pins are grouped together on "boards" as if they were actual pin boards.

Pinterest users are overwhelmingly female. This means that if you run a sports bar with a mostly male customer base, Pinterest may not be for you.

When a user shares another's pin it is called a repin, just like retweeting or reblogging. Pins can be shared via Twitter and Facebook, a feature that lends itself well to running a multi-channeled campaign.

Unlike other social media services that have a relatively level playing field in terms of number of users that are male or female, 80% of Pinterest users are women, with over 90% of the pins that are created and shared being done so by women[13]. This is an important statistic to know; if you run a sports bar with an overwhelmingly male customer base, Pinterest may not be for you.

The good news is that Pinterest is a commerce aligned platform. This means that users are used to being the subject of marketing and have almost come to expect it. Experts in the field of social media marketing agree that commercial content is less at odds with the behavior of Pinterest users than other social networking sites which is good news all around for businesses.

Food is in the top five on both the list of top ten Pinterest categories and top ten board names. This means that you will really have to pull out the stops photographing

---

[13] Source: Marketing Land "Report: 92% of Pinterest Pins made by Women" Greg Sterling May 12, 2014 marketingland.com

your entrées and drinks. Many brands have discovered that the true strength with Pinterest lies in sharing a lifestyle, not just pictures of their product. This is a well-known fact for many marketing professionals but it hits home with leveraging Pinterest.

Of course you will share pictures. Everyone is sharing pictures. And the fact that everyone is doing it means that yours need to stand out. Many users find inspiration for craft projects and fashion styles through Pinterest. Harness that need with elaborate presentations of enticing entrées and decadent desserts. Cocktails should be artfully prepared with creative garnishes and everyone, absolutely everyone needs to be smiling.

Another step in the creation of a lifestyle concept is the invitation of influential guest pinners. These could be celebrities who have eaten at your establishment, professional cooks, chefs, or even users who are popular within the sphere of Pinterest. Just because a fashion and style guru doesn't pin pictures of food doesn't mean that her followers don't eat. The more popular the figure, the higher the chances that a potential customer in your area will be following them,

Of course celebrities may say no. What you use to entice them to "guest pin" is between the two of you, but be persistent. Even letting people who are following you guest pin recipes and pictures of their own food could work with your brand and your demographic. Not so much if you're a wine bar, probably a better fit for a family restaurant (50% of Pinterest users have children[14]).

Pinterest can also be used to tell your brand's story. Consider using "candid" photos, photos that show the human side of your brand as opposed to just your logo, food, and staff on the job. Photos of "business birthday parties" or events that commemorate the founding of the restaurant can contribute to your brand's timeline and also serve a dual purpose of thanking your followers. Photos labelled "The Corner Pub turns 10 today! We're celebrating with a big slice of cake and a BIG glass of wine" depicting a decadent cake and a novelty oversized wine glass. In

---

[14] Source: "10 Most Popular Categories and Board Names on Pinterest" Brandon Gaille June 22, 2013 brandongaille.com

the post, link to your website or blog where you have a recipe for the house cake or the cake pictured and make wine pairing recommendations.

If it hasn't become clear up to this point, let me say it outright. Your interactions on social media should create value for the people that you interact with. Standing out from your competitors let alone the crowd is absolutely key to getting noticed and retain your followers and fans. Providing value to your followers, customers, and peers that you network with online ensures that they pay attention to what you have to offer and listen to what you have to say.

Putting it All Together

-1-

The first step of all aspects of a social media campaign is of course to set goals. This may seem like a broken record at this point but the value of goal setting should never be discounted when it comes to planning and strategy.

Pinterest is, at heart, a photo sharing and trend generating site. That means telling your brand's story visually and showing off your establishment and brand in a creative way. A following on Pinterest should be viewed the same way as other social media channels in the sense that it is a funnel that drives users to your website and ultimately to your establishment.

-2-

Create your Pinterest profile. Pinterest allows users to create business pages to showcase their brand. While this system is designed to primarily drive shopping sales it is a powerful force for all businesses. Once your profile is created and verified brand it with your logo, cover photo and bio. Add the "Pin It" button to your website or blog to allow users to add your content to their pin board so they can go back and look at it later. Pinterest provides the drop-in code to add your Pin It button.

-3-

Get going with content. Use eye-catching and creative photos and content that is value-added for your customers, and stick to one theme. Remember not to start promoting your page until you have enough content for a complete page.

-4-

Use Pinterest analytics. Pinterest provides an entire set of analytics and insights for business pages so you can learn more about the people pinning you. Use this information to make the best kind of decisions (informed decisions) about the direction of your campaign on Pinterest.

Pinterest recommends that good pins have three basic characteristics. Pins should be:

- Helpful – **Pins should be informative and add value to users' lives.**

- Beautiful – **Pins should be compelling, attractive, and creative to engage more users.**

- Actionable – **Pins should help users take action on their interests**

Pinterest also recommends building curated lists or picking a number of items to compile into a list that saves users time searching out the individual components themselves. An example would be a list of "8 Mouthwateringly Unique Mac & Cheese Recipes".

The concept of content curation is not limited to Pinterest, though it is a natural fit for that platform. Content curation is the act of compiling different, related content and maintaining it in a single collection. Effective content curation can be a solid brand asset; people will begin to associate your brand with the one-stop shop it has become for all of their online content consumption needs.

A word of warning concerning content curation however; it is an easy distraction. Devoting your valuable time to amassing, maintaining, and updating a collection of content can divert your attention from other goals and can dilute your brand and marketing efforts. Curate with care.

Quick Review

- ✓ **Pinterest is designed to be a virtual** pin board. **Posts are called** pins **and are grouped together in** boards.

- ✓ Pins **act as bookmarks that link back to your content.**

- ✓ **While Pinterest is a business friendly environment, there is also an expectation and fierce competition between brands to provide** value-added **content in the form of pins.**

- ✓ Content curation **can be an effective way to build extensive collections of value-added content but the drive to accumulate and update can become a distraction.**

Estimated number of U.S. Pinterest users in 2015: 47.1 million

14.2 minutes is the average duration of each Pinterest visit

98 minutes is the average accumulated duration of visits to Pinterest

Percentage of Americans that use Pinterest during work hours

Percentage of U.S. adults that use Pinterest

Percentage of Pinterest users that are from outside the U.S.

LinkedIn

prospects, professionals, and potential

LinkedIn is the world's largest professional network. Currently, this business oriented social media platform has over 350 million members[15] and is dedicated to "connect[ing] the world's professionals to make them more productive and successful". This self-described mission is what sets LinkedIn apart from other social media services. Platforms like Facebook are for casual connections; friends, off the clock coworker interaction, family, and neighbors. LinkedIn is one of the few social networking sites an office employee may be able to access on the clock, normally checking your Facebook page is considered poor efficiency in a productivity oriented environment.

While it's true that many of your customers may have LinkedIn accounts, especially if they're working professionals, your LinkedIn account will be less of a customer engagement channel and more of a business development and networking channel.

---

[15] Source: "By the Numbers: 125+ Amazing LinkedIn Statistics" Craig Smith May 4, 2015 expandedramblings.com

That being said, there are some creative ways that LinkedIn users have leveraged their channels, and we'll get to that in a moment after we examine some of the primary business networking benefits that LinkedIn offers.

- Finding talent **is a great utilization of LinkedIn's service and represents one of the organic uses of the platform. To put that another way, LinkedIn was designed to match employers with a pool of motivated talent.**

- Keeping pace with industry trends**, developments, and updates is easier too. Small business development organizations, restaurant advocates, and industry leaders all have LinkedIn profiles they use to communicate with like-minded business owners.**

- Developing business relationships **with new suppliers, promoters, and marketers is easy to do in LinkedIn's purpose built environment. Alcohol suppliers and brands understand that LinkedIn's professional community represents the larger part of their target market; above the legal drinking age, disposable** income, and trying to relax after a stressful day. Hint, this is largely your target market too.

Because LinkedIn is such a developed community for professionals and employers alike, when scouting for new talent LinkedIn is a tremendous resources. Once you have created an account with LinkedIn, your email contacts can be imported and you can request to connect with people you already know. Through this network you may be introduced to new people who have the skills you're looking for, but maybe not. You can always search based on keywords, geographic locality, etc... to find professional servers, bartenders, social media directors, restaurant and bar managers and so on.

You know that your people are a huge asset, probably your biggest unless you have a location that is a kingmaker regardless of the food and staff. If you have been in the business long enough you know that the restaurant industry has a high level turnover when it comes to staff, both reliable and unreliable. Building a

LinkedIn profile that is a magnet for top-quality employees means that you will have the pick of the bunch when hiring to replace attrition or to expand your staff.

Keeping up with the ever evolving industry surrounding your business is critical. Assume that your competitors are doing it too and you don't want to be left behind. If they're not doing it, then score one for your team. Your competitors can be a critical part of your industry research; seeing what they're doing with their LinkedIn profiles is a huge asset to you. Replicate what you like and use your creativity and passion to enhance it to attract better talent to your brand and build your reputation.

LinkedIn is a way for you to establish your brand's credibility. No matter how many tweets, posts, or photos you post your peers will only see what you want your customers to when they access your other social media channels. The content that you produce to engage your customers and drive sales is does not necessarily convey the information that you need to establish business relationships.

The service is divided in two between personal profiles and company pages. Just like Facebook, in order to create a company page, first you must have a personal profile. Even if you had no intention of creating a personal profile on LinkedIn this is a good thing. While people can follow your business page, your personal connections will also be working to expand your network.

When creating your company page, the bare necessities include a company name, email address, a website URL and short bio. Obviously we're going to go above and beyond that minimum. There are some other requirements that must first be addressed when creating your company page: your personal profile must be Intermediate strength or higher. LinkedIn uses a scale to show the completeness of personal profiles which reflects the amount of information contained in your profile.

When it comes to developing your personal profile on LinkedIn the more info you provide the better. A headshot, resume, list of skills, importing your email contacts will all contribute to your completeness level.

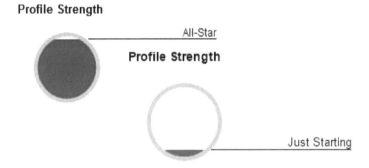

Figure 11 The highest and lowest levels of LinkedIn profile completeness. Note that even though the All-Star rating has space left inside the icon, it is the highest level of completeness a profile can achieve.

Once that's all taken care of you can create and build your company page. The ins and outs of your company page are covered in the "putting it all together" portion of this chapter, here we will continue to explore the capabilities of LinkedIn.

Developing relationships with peers and others in your industry is arguably the reason LinkedIn exists. Suppliers and other B2B (business to business) companies realize that LinkedIn is the place that they will find their prospects, leads, and sales; therefore they are searching LinkedIn for clients. It may sound silly to say that joining LinkedIn is a good way to get pitched for a sale but the truth of the matter is you have an opportunity to shop around for suppliers and other business partners who will be competing for your business.

For catering companies and restaurants that cater, inserting yourself into local discussions concerning meetings, events, and catering opportunities could produce leads that translate into business. Remember not to push sales within LinkedIn groups however, it is more important to add productive value to professional conversations to preserve the integrity of your brand. Letting prospects know you are available and that your food is top-notch can have much more of a positive effect than blasting your connections with coupons.

Because LinkedIn is professional network, business improvement information abounds and much of it is free. With my own LinkedIn account I performed a simple search and located libraries of information ranging from menu design tips and increasing menu profitability to workforce utilization and management techniques.

In addition to the raw information, new insights can be gained from group discussions and interaction, and all of the article authors have their own LinkedIn profiles. It has been my experience that many of these people are more than willing to answer questions and partake in discussions concerning the material that have written.

-1-

Identify your goals for your LinkedIn page. Remember, LinkedIn is a business oriented networking service. This means that it can be a recruitment tool, a way to stay current within the restaurant industry, and develop relationships with new suppliers. Business to business companies routinely use LinkedIn to generate leads and your exposure to them means that you can shop around for the partner that is a best fit for your business.

-2-

Create your LinkedIn page. In order to do so you will need to meet some minimum requirements with a personal profile to administer the page. Use an engaging, eye-catching photo for your banner image and write a concise and honest bio. Remember that your LinkedIn page will be a one-stop shop for visitors seeking information about your business so the more complete your page the more impactful your presence on the LinkedIn channel will be.

The more complete your profile, the easier it will be to find. As you add more material, the higher your page will rank in LinkedIn search results. Add links to your other social media channels and add company specialties on your company page. Don't forget photos and videos as well to tell your brand's story and show your peers who you are.

-3-

Participate in conversations. Throw your two cents in with discussions and be genuinely helpful, not pushing your brand or your image. Encourage followers and others to write reviews, respond to comments that are questions and pose your own comments as questions to strike up conversations.

All of these tactics are designed to grow your network through followers, or people with other professional contacts. Consider those you follow and those who follow you as resources, but don't view the relationship as a quid pro quo situation; no one likes to be data mined or taken advantage of.

-4-

Use LinkedIn to monitor your competitors. See who they are following and talking to. If they are participating in a conversation regarding the industry, you should know what they know about it. Use LinkedIn groups to find like-minded businesses and business owners locally and globally both non-competing and competition alike. Of course, focusing on local discussions will yield the best results and it will be the area that you can have the highest level of impact. Mention your connections by name in posts or conversations to let them know you're talking about them and that you value their input. Remember to contribute to the conversation in a meaningful way.

Unlike other social media platforms, LinkedIn is better utilized to develop relationships, not accumulate the highest number of connections. This goes back to the idea of treating your connections like resources. LinkedIn places value on the endorsements of your closest connections not to mention the opportunity value of developing relationships with peers.

- ✓ **LinkedIn is a** business oriented **social media networking service.**

- ✓ **LinkedIn is a purpose-built** recruiting tool **as well as a** professional networking **platform.**

- ✓ **LinkedIn is a fantastic tool to** track industry trends **and** monitor **the efforts of your competitors.**

- ✓ **Because of the business oriented nature of LinkedIn,** joining the conversation **can yield important insights into the industry and develop personal and brand level relationships.**

Content Sharing
Services

YouTube, Flickr, and the world of

video and photo sharing

So far we've been looking at social media sites that are largely networking in nature. We'll wrap up our examination of popular social media platforms with two services that are purpose built for the sharing of content. Of course there is a networking element here too; the goal of many users is to create and share content that is truly viral. Let's take a look at how video-sharing platform YouTube and photo-sharing network Flickr can be used to tell your brand's story visually.

YouTube

YouTube is an Internet phenomenon in addition to being far and away the most popular video sharing social network. YouTube has over 1 billion users per month, a number which YouTube's owner Google claims accounts for one out of every two people on the Internet[16]. That is truly massive. You may know YouTube as the number one spot on the Web to find videos of dogs on skateboards, cats, and people irresponsibly using fireworks but YouTube represents a huge opportunity for businesses.

---

[16] Source: "YouTube Stats: Site Has Over 1 Billion Users Each Month" Reuters March 21, 2013 Huffington Post

The power and size of YouTube comes from its crowdsourcing capacity. Anyone can upload a video of nearly anything and have people talking about it instantly. With the proliferation and ubiquity of smart devices with video recording capability more and more events and moments of our lives are being recorded, archived, and uploaded.

Using YouTube as a method of marketing narrows the platform's scope considerably. The following list summarizes the ways in which YouTube can be used to bolster your social media campaign.

- Generate traffic **to your website with links and engaging content. Traffic to your website means traffic to your squeeze page and access to all of the ways that you entice customers to patronize your establishment.**

- Build your brand **and generate interest and buzz. While someone from across the globe stumbling upon your video may not translate into money in** your pocket YouTube as a host for your videos is free, reliable, trusted, and above all easy.

- Contribute positively to your SEO (**search engine optimization) and social media reach by adding content for your Google Places account (and thereby raising its rank) as well as branded content that can show up in other searches. YouTube videos can be embedded into websites and blogs for on demand content.**

Let's go over some of the terms associated with YouTube. YouTube calls its accounts channels which is slightly confusing since the marketing term for our social media accounts (and traditional methods of marketing) is channels.

Your channel is your profile. Other users can subscribe to your channel which is in effect "following" your account. Subscribers see all of the content you produce. Below each of your videos there is space for users to leave comments or responses to your video. A popular method of response is to leave a video response or to produce another YouTube video as a comment on an existing video. The video response will show up in the comments section of the video. Groups of videos can be organized into playlists that will play a series of videos one after the other.

The term "embed" has come up a couple of times so far. YouTube offers users the opportunity to embed videos into their websites and blogs. To embed, click the icon and copy and paste the lines of code generated into the code for your website in the appropriate place.

YouTube is powered by Google. This means that your Google account is all you need to start a profile. Your channel landing page will have the option to add a profile picture and the equivalent of a cover photo. Take this opportunity do some creative visual branding and fill out a bio.

YouTube is so video-packed that the amount of content is truly staggering. Because we're trying to drive traffic to our website and our establishment, engaging in extensive YouTube SEO isn't necessary. People don't log on to YouTube to find a great local Italian restaurant. That doesn't mean YouTube has no value for the restaurant and bar industry; all that means is that we have to stretch the YouTube platform to fit our needs, and we will use YouTube to boost our SEO elsewhere, namely through Google+ and Google Places.

There are many ways to upload and host video, but given the size, reach, and ubiquity of YouTube it should be your first choice. Size means reliability, ubiquity means trust. Plus, YouTube interfaces seamlessly with the Google suite. But why shoot video in the first place?

I'm not going to tell you to shoot the next big blockbuster. Short videos are a good choice and fall into two categories: branded promotional, and branded value-added. Branded promotional videos are fairly straightforward and are like short TV commercials. These creative shorts are used to tell your customers about your brand, your establishment, and how much fun a pleasurable dining experience at your restaurant can be. Shoot one to embed on your website, post to Facebook and use YouTube to upload and host it.

Branded value-added are a little different. These videos range in length from well under a minute to however long it takes to convey your message. These videos are not about your establishment per say, but provide value to your customers. Use these videos as you would branded promotional material, but like forums, blog posts, and many of your tweets or posts these videos provide information, tips and tricks, or recipes that enrich your customers' lives while improving your brand perception. Examples would be a short video entitled "How to Make Restaurant Quality Moist Chicken Every Time!" or "10 Tricks to Use in the Kitchen to Speed up Prep".

Quality of videos and cost are interdependent here; the better a video, potentially the more it will cost. Always

try produce the highest quality video you can afford.
Cheesy videos do little to improve your brand perception.

Putting it All Together

-1-

Establish goals for your YouTube channel. Will you use it just as an uploader and host for video content that will be shared and embedded or will you develop your YouTube channel into a method of reaching out to customers?

-2-

Create your YouTube channel. Brand your page with a bio, logo, and cover photo. If you will be sharing your YouTube channel, wait until you have content and playlists before getting the word out. A skeleton profile on any social media platform can scare away customers and reflects poorly on your brand as unprofessional. You should always strive to build a complete profile for any social media channel that you participate in, no matter the level of exposure you expect.

Upload videos, the more the better. This does not mean flood your profile with ten second clips of your dishwasher dropping a tray of plates, but upload branded promotional and branded-value added videos. Build playlists of related videos. To expand your value-added capacity to your customers include the videos of other users that fit your brand's image, target demographic, produce helpful content.

This is one of the great features about marketing on YouTube. The fact that the entire platform is user-generated and the enormous user base means there is no shortage of content. You can build playlists (read: content curation) that feature the material of other users, just don't claim it's yours. Give credit where credit is due and always treat the owners of the material with respect. If they ask you to remove material from a playlist it is often a good idea to comply and look for replacement material elsewhere. There is no advantage to fighting other users for content and the negative PR storm that can accompany a drawn out fight.

Once you have a well-developed YouTube channel spread the word. Cross promoting your YouTube channel on other social media channels will drive traffic to your channel but remember, the channel should drive traffic to your website and establishment as well. Use YouTube's embed feature to incorporate your videos into your website or blog and remember that YouTube comments are now linked into Google+. When determining whether to use YouTube as a driver of traffic it is a good idea to consider how that will work in tandem with your Google+ account should you choose to leverage that platform.

Quick Review

- ✓ **YouTube profiles are called** channels. **Channels can be branded with your logo, bio, and cover photo. Followers on YouTube are known as** subscribers.

- ✓ **YouTube is owned by** Google. **YouTube interfaces with** Google+ **and one login is needed for access to the entire Google suite.**

✓ Similar videos can be organized into playlists. Playlists can contain videos from other users so consider blending your videos with the videos of others to add value to the experience of your subscribers.

✓ Consider the two types of video that you can upload; branded promotional **and** branded value-added. **Promotional videos act as commercials that advertise your brand's story or promote your product while value-added videos contribute to your brand perception and enrich the lives of your customers, incentivizing them to subscribe to your channel.**

✓ Use other social media channels to promote your YouTube channel. Use YouTube's embed feature to host YouTube videos on your website or blog.

Flickr

Flickr (pronounced "flicker") is a photo and video sharing site that was acquired by Yahoo! in 2005. The service acts as a way for users to collect, share, display collections of photos and video. Popular for visually heavy industries, Flickr has an artistic slant and a large number of photo blogs. In this capacity, Flickr can act in much the same way Tumblr does (other than both names missing a vowel) for businesses. Photos that have been uploaded can be accessed by those without an account which is a handy feature of the platform. Of course to upload photos, an account must be created.

Flickr offers three types of accounts: Free, Ad Free, and Doublr. The Free account is more than adequate for most casual users. It provides a 1 Terabyte of storage space for photos not more than 200 MB in size and videos not more than 3 minutes or 1 GB each. Ad Free provides the same features but enhances the Flickr browsing experience by suppressing ads for an annual fee. The Doublr level account is a super-premium account for photography professionals. At time of publication the price tag on a

Flickr Doublr account is $499, making it the most expensive expression of social media I have encountered. Doublr accounts double the provided storage space to 2 Terabytes.

Users on Flickr see their photos organized into a "photostream". This can be viewed in a number of ways and if your account's privacy settings allow it (and it will if you're trying to get the word out) other users can tag your photos as you would tag them yourself. Photos can be organized into "albums", a more flexible and robust method of organization than a traditional "file folder" system. Photos can belong to one, multiple, or no album(s) simultaneously and the massive amount of storage space offered to Free users permits the upload of approximately 500,000 photos that retain every pixel of their original resolution.

Flickr users can create and join groups which is a great way to get your content seen by more sets of eyes. One uploaded to a group only you and the group administrator can remove the photo. A word of caution for non-photography businesses looking to use Flickr as a marketing channel; because of the high level of artistic expression on Flickr and the number of photographers and artists, "sales pitch" photos may receive negative comments or tags.

Flickr is obviously oriented for visual content. It is a community designed to expedite the sharing, storage, and consumption of visual content. The platform provides lines of code for embedding photos into websites and blogs as well as the option to share to other social media channels straight from your photostream. If Flickr is so photo and art oriented, how is it pertinent to this book? Let's take a look.

Flickr may not be a good choice for a sports bar or dive bar. Motivated business owners and managers who have an interest in photography can leverage the platform by taking artistic shots of their establishments, food, ingredients, and locale. This is not for everyone but a good photographer can build a photo album out of nearly any subject. Flickr offers an on demand wall art and photo book production service that can transform photos from your collection into living, breathing wall art. Of course there's no accounting for taste but a professionally shot inspirational gallery on the wall of your bistro, of your bistro is a trendy self-branding option.

To look at Flickr in a different way, let's look at the way that photography can help develop a brand with various subject and theme choices. You know your customers and your target demographic. Keep that info at the forefront of your mind when looking over this list as some projects are more impactful for some demographics and less impactful for others.

1. Take artistic photos of your establishment, your food, and willing customers. **These photos can be uploaded to Flickr, and geotagged with the location of your restaurant. Your photo collection can**

become value-added content for your customers and social media fans and followers.

2. Take artistic photos of the city or town around your establishment. **Not only can these photos be shared on Flickr and other social media channels but a project like this can be leveraged to improve a brand's "neighborhood eatery" perception. Coffee shops, cafés, bistros, and wine bars are all excellent candidates for local photography campaigns.**

3. Combine elements of the previous two Flickr projects and use the platform's wall art and photo book production feature to decorate your establishment with self-generated photography. **In neighborhood restaurants walls covered with gallery style and professional photography can improve atmosphere and neighborhood engagement. Self-produced wall décor also allows you to select exactly the content and fine tune your atmosphere and brand perception.**

Cafés with lounge, communal, and coffee table seating can leave self-generated photo books as

coffee table books for customers. These photo books will elevate brand perception and refine your position as an establishment on the cutting edge of trends.

Also consider creating and sharing digital photobooks to entice customers to your website (and squeeze page). If your taste is in line with theirs they will subscribe to your email mailing list to experience the value you provide through photographic expression.

The word "artistic" was used frequently in the previous list and that was no accident. Labeling photos as art can be murky waters and can potentially open your brand up to increased criticism and scrutiny. On the other hand, art as a marketing tool is no new concept and it is here to stay. Because of the discerning nature of Flickr users and the high quality standards you have in place for the atmosphere of your business, be picky with the subjects and the photos you select.

Flickr can of course be used to share the same kinds of photos you have been sharing on Facebook, Instagram, etc... but doing so is not leveraging the platform to its fullest potential. A quick exploration of Flickr will show the high caliber of photos other users are sharing and the need to stand out and be creative immediately becomes apparent.

Putting it All Together

-1-

Establish goals for your presence on Flickr. Remember, Flickr is completely photo-centric. Social networking and community interaction is based around the photos so a profile with weak photography will be passed over. Think ahead to the end game. Will you be generating wall art or photobooks for your establishment? Will your Flickr account be a part of a larger neighborhood engagement campaign through photography?

-2-

Create an account. Flickr is owned by Yahoo! so a Yahoo! Mail account gets you in. Select a user name that reflects your brand, upload a cover photo and complete all the bio information. Don't start sharing your profile until you have a robust photostream and some albums.

-3-

Upload photos to fill your photostream and create albums. Upload photos that fit your plan and take steps to fulfill your goals. In addition to the aforementioned list, consider creating an album that visually tells the story of your brand as you would with other visual content sharing services but remember the artistic direction that Flickr leans.

-4-

Join groups and become part of the discussion. Groups can be created based on a number of different criteria. As you develop a position within Flickr use your participation in the discussion to gain credibility you can later use to solidify your brand's position as a friend to the arts within your community. Excerpts from community discussions can be included in email blasts, blog posts and on your website to provide value and superior brand image to your customers.

Consider creating a new group that focuses on your geographic area and local themes for photo subjects. This will promote your brand as a thought leader in the neighborhood when it comes to local photography and being trend-forward.

Flickr is something of a niche social media application and that should be kept in the forefront of your mind when making decisions regarding your Flickr participation. Like other social media services, Flickr requires a steady stream of input to become an asset to be leveraged and that content needs to be better than your average photo. A solid commitment to Flickr is best done with a surplus of time on your hands or better yet with a dedicated social media director, freelance photographer, or graphic designer none of whom work for minimum wage. Planning and a long-term goal are essential components of an effective Flickr presence.

Quick Review

✓ **Uploaded photos on Flickr are added to a user's** photostream. **Photos can be organized into** albums.

✓ **Flickr is highly photo-centric and has a high proportion of** artists and photographers. **Keep this in mind when generating content.**

✓ **Photos on Flickr can be turned into on demand** wall art and coffee table books **which lend a trendy addition to certain establishments.**

Making Sense of
Social Media

a summary of your social media
campaign

We know that setting goals and making plans is an integral part of the social media campaign but that's really only half of the equation. Measuring your social media campaign has to take into account a number of different metrics including but not even close to being limited to likes, followers, retweets, hashtag trending, and reviews.

Making sense of all of these boils down to the ultimate goal: making money for your business. A social media marketing campaign is no different than any other business decision in this sense. As a business owner, manager, or decision maker you decided to spend money to make money for your establishment. Social media campaigns don't have to be costly; all of the platforms we have covered in this book are free to join. That being said, almost all of them have a premium service oriented for businesses whether in the form of ad generation or automated campaigns.

The biggest investment into social media campaigns is almost always time, which if the popular saying is to be believed is exactly the same as money. Time can sometimes be even scarcer for small business owners than money and that is doubly true for the restaurant and bar industry. Since time is a resource we can never get back, measuring ROI becomes of paramount importance.

ROI measurement isn't just looking at a report that says "Your thirty hours of input have given you $2,345 in added revenue." It is a much more complex tool that that can tell you which efforts are paying off, which aren't making any money, and the stability and success of your campaign (or any business undertaking).

Running a social media campaign requires focus, and in the struggle to develop your marketing channels it can be easy to lose sight of the focus on ROI. While this doesn't mean that your business will burst into flames it does mean that you could be wasting time and money or failing to optimize programs that are winners. Keeping ROI in the front of your mind while planning and measuring your social media campaign.

Sounds great right? The next question is of course "How do I measure my social media campaign?" Let's take a look.

In order to measure anything the first step is to set goals. To use the same example from earlier in the chapter, if you have generated $2,345 in added revenue from thirty hours of input what does that number tell us? Nothing really. It is informative because it reports a condition but there is very little to be learned from that statement by itself.

If, however, in the last measured period thirty hours of input generated $3,117 in added revenue then the above number represents a downward trend. Conversely, if in the last measured period thirty hours of input yielded $1,946 then you are trending upward. Generally speaking, upward trends as far as added revenue are going to be the kind that are in line with goals (am I right?).

So without context, individual measurements don't mean very much and without goals or objectives they don't mean much. When creating a social media campaign it is important to identify the kind of traffic and sales you are trying to produce. Do you want a campaign that drives immediate traffic into your establish or do you want one that helps build future traffic and sales?

You're reading this book because you have a bar, restaurant, or café and you're saying "Yes to all." While that may be the overall goal, smaller goals and a narrower focus are necessary to get the most out of your campaign. As your campaign matures and your brand has a more stable relationship with the people you interact with on social media channels developing short and long terms sales together becomes possible. Take a look at the following recommendations.

1. Start with a campaign that focuses on developing your brand perception. Brands need to develop brand magnetism or qualities that will make their brands appealing for people to be involved with. Tell your story, provide value, and don't focus a hard-selling your customers. As you develop brand magnetism it will be easier to streamline your selling process.

2. Start with a focus on building desire for your menu items, service, and atmosphere. Focusing on driving future sales and developing your brand will make loyal customers more receptive to later campaigns that focus on immediacy.

3. Leverage channels for their time-based characteristics. Twitter has such high turnover and such little permanence that it is an excellent channel for campaigns designed to drive short-term and immediate business. Facebook on the other hand has a much higher degree of permanence and is better suited to longer-term, repeat customer, and brand loyalty development. We'll talk about which platforms to select out of the multitude the next section of this chapter.

4. A campaign that has a narrow focus is easier to track that one that is trying to be everything for everyone. It makes more sense to have narrow goals for each channel and focus your efforts accordingly.

5. Don't try to measure everything. You will get bogged down with an information overload if you try to measure the minutia of your campaigns; each like, follower, retweet, etc...

6. Use your measurements, compare them to goals and track your progress. There is no point measuring if you're not using the data and there's no point setting goals if you won't be tracking your progress toward those goals. As your campaign matures you may find that there are metrics that you have been tracking diligently that aren't that useful anymore. It's fine to stop tracking those metrics if they are no longer helpful and be on the lookout for other progress indicators.

ROI

Quality

Quantity

Social media campaigns can be measured in three distinct ways.

The world data-gathering side of social media is nearly purely quantitative, meaning that this data is expressed as numbers or statistics. This is good info to have and it can assist in the determinations of the other two methods of measurement.

Qualitative measurement is less numbers-driven and more

attribute and character determined. Qualitative

measurement is more aligned with the thoughts, emotions and opinions of your customers.

Measurement of ROI is the big one. These measurements show profit generated, number of customers attracted, and number of customers retained.

Quantitative

Quantitative measurement represents the volume of traffic your brand is generating. This could be Twitter followers, Facebook fans, or traffic to your business website. There are a number of tools in addition to the free insights provided by many social media sites. All social media platforms have built-in insights that are accurate and easily accessed, though some are more comprehensive than others.

Google Analytics is a fan favorite in this area and probably the most sensible for a restaurant or bar owner. Google Analytics provides you with a drop-in line of code and measures numerous metrics regarding traffic on your website.

Other software packages in this area get pricey fast but deliver the ability to efficiently and intelligently analyze truly massive amounts of data. While these programs have a place for ecommerce sites, many bars and restaurants have little use for the high-powered analytics and little interest in the high price tag.

A side note about your competitor's traffic: there are web tools designed to measure and compare traffic across several sites. Compete.com has a free version and a broad scope though there are other, very effective options that exist.

Knowing how many people are looking into is good information to have but software extensions exist that can track what they're saying about you as well. Google Alerts is a great tool in this category; once established it can be set up to email you daily reports of the online conversations people are having about your brand. Don't stop there though, why not make one of the keywords the name of a competitor's brand to receive daily reports of what people are saying about them? Other services exist in this category too: Spiral16, SocialMention, and Alterian SM2 to mention a few.

Qualitative

Qualitative measurement is also a critical component of the ROI measurement process and contributes valuable decision-making information. A tried and true method of obtaining qualitative information is with surveys. Surveys are nothing new to the world of bars and restaurants; a well-crafted survey can determine important insights about a customer's dining experience in ways he or she may not have been able to articulate directly. Surveys are easy and effective to use with a variety of survey-creation software and Q&A type site plug-ins.

Question such as the following can guide customer responses. Remember to use specific language when creating a survey and only introduce one topic per question.

How did you hear about our Facebook page?

We have accounts with Facebook, Twitter, Google+, and Instagram. Is there another service where you would like to see us?

Which social media service(s) do you use most often?

Standard survey creation software will aggregate and organize the results for easy interpretation. Don't forget to incentivize your customers, fans, and followers to take the survey with gift cards or coupons.

An alternative option to the use of outbound surveys is the creation of a forum where users can ask questions and discuss topics with you and with one another. Here it is especially necessary to provide value in the form of helpful articles, recipes, and deals etc... as participation in a forum is much more time consumptive than taking a single survey.

Programs like Social Radar track, measure, and analyze conversation from all over the web. This program also

provides insights into key emotional words surrounding the conversation and can help you track why people are happy or upset with your brand.

Calculating your ROI

In order to calculate the return on your investment the first step is to determine a customer lifetime value number. Your CLV numbers are based on average check dollar amounts and the frequency with which your customers become the best kind of customers (repeat customers).

Let's say that your average check is $34.50 and your average customer eats at your establishment four times a month, year round.   This means that you have a CLV of $1,656 ($34.50 x (4 monthly visits x 12 months)). The next step is to calculate your allowable CPA (cost per acquisition) or the budgeted cost of attracting customers to your business. Experts agree that ten percent of your CLV is a good baseline number to use when calculating what your marketing budget per customer is. In this example, the CPA would be $165.60 per year ($1,656 x 10%). The restaurant business is fortunate in this respect since there are a certain number of "freebie" walk-ins and the potential for wildly varying check amounts based on party size, menu items ordered, drinks etc... While this number may be hard to nail down and you may experiment with reducing (or increasing) your **CPA** budget it serves as a good base benchmark against which to gauge your marketing and advertising budget.

This is a *marketing* budget, so that figure includes your traditional channels of marketing as well. To narrow down and compare two channels directly use surveys, track exclusive coupons, and poll customers to see what encouraged them to come in.

An important aspect of all of these calculations is to thoroughly research and expose your hidden costs. Attach a value to the time that you spend establishing and maintaining a social media campaign and use that number when assessing time-saving and efficiency related purchases (such as new tracking software). We know by now that though signing up for Facebook or Twitter is free, the workload involved with running those (and other) channels is hefty.

The good news: if you take your time, plan ahead, and spend the money, your online and social media marketing campaign will be an asset for your brand.

The not so good news: if you don't do any of the above you can waste time, effort, and money with little to show for it.

Knowing Which Services to Use

There's a lot of social media platforms out there. More than listed here. Way more. Social media is here to stay, and it's not limited to English. The world's second largest social media site, with 720 million users is China's QZone[17]. That's more than Twitter and Instagram combined. For a pizza shop in Sacramento perhaps QZone is a poor fit.

---

[17] Source: "Check Out the Numbers on China's Top 10 Social Media Sites (Infographic) Steven Millward March 13, 2013 Tech in Asia www.techinasia.com

That does however raise the question, which services do I use? That's ultimately up to you, your business model, your demographics, and your budget. To make the best kind of decision (an informed one) let's revisit what we know about various services.

Facebook

Facebook is the go-to social networking service for many online users. As a result it is a great channel to use for spreading the word regarding your establishment, other social media channels, website, coupons, promotions, and events.

Like all social media interaction, Facebook users demand value-added content and will reward such content with likes. Your Facebook page (different from a personal profile remember) also acts as an archive of sorts where other users can browse your timeline to see content you posted in the past. Many other social media services integrate with Facebook so as you develop a presence on other channels you can promote posts with links that automatically post to Facebook for you.

Twitter

Twitter is a time-sensitive microblogging platform where interaction is made up of 140 character exchanges called tweets. Tweets are transient, meaning they have a high probability of being missed. Twitter requires a stream of tweets daily to remain current with your followers. Extensions like TweetDeck allow you to schedule tweets in advance to streamline the process.

Twitter's timeliness can be leveraged to take advantage of time-based opportunities such as surplus inventory or slow-traffic evenings. Plus, other Twitter users' tweets can be shared via retweet a way to blend your content with value-added content of other users. Produce content in addition to promotions that will get retweeted to expand your reach to new groups of people.

Instagram

Instagram is (at date of publication) a mobile-only platform. It focuses on taking and sharing photos that are displayed in a characteristic square portrait instead of the usual smart device 4:3 ratio. Owned by Facebook, Instagram is growing rapidly and is becoming an increasingly profitable platform for businesses that integrates seamlessly with Facebook's platform.

Instagram is best used to tell your brand's story visually, a current and successful trend in the social media marketing industry. Photos can be tagged with hashtags that group them with similar photos and make them searchable within the platform. Customer engagement can be driven through photo and hashtag contests.

Google+

Google+ represents Google's offering to the world of social media. Though relatively new, the platform has been steadily been gaining popularity since its inception. Google+ interfaces with other Google products like AdWords, analytics, Places, and My Business.

One of the great features of Google+ is that it allows you to break your followers up into "circles" or specific groups. Content can be posted to separate circles and therefore can be tailored to each circle's demographic.

Tumblr

Tumblr is a rapidly growing micro- and short-blogging site. The platform's focus is on the production and curation of a variety of different media types with a focus on humor and creativity. High quality content is frequently reblogged so the pressure is on for brands that want to create viral material on Tumblr.

Pinterest

Pinterest is a platform made up of pins or bookmarks that link back to your material. Pins are organized into groups called boards, a shout out to the platform's concept of being a virtual pin board. Pinterest's user base is overwhelmingly female which is an important statistic to know when deciding if Pinterest is right for your brand.

Pinterest is very business friendly but it does put pressure on companies that participate to produce high quality value-added content that is appealing to users. To streamline the pinning process, Pinterest does provide lines of code to produce your own "pin it" button that can be dropped into your website or blog.

LinkedIn

LinkedIn is a social network of business professionals. It is useful in acquiring talent, adding credibility to your brand's image, and developing supplier and other business relationships. LinkedIn is a great platform to mine for opportunity but the focus of the service is not business to consumer interaction but B2B contact and employee acquisition.

Content Sharing Services

YouTube is easily the go-to service for video-hosting and –sharing. Owned by Google, YouTube interfaces with the Google suite seamlessly. YouTube is a reliable and trusted channel for your brand to upload video that either promotes your brand, food, and service or adds value to the lives of your subscribers. Build a playlist that blends your content with content from others to provide a richer experience for your subscribers. Use YouTube's embed feature to share your videos on your blog, website, and other social media channels.

Flickr is a photo storage and sharing service owned by Yahoo!. Flickr focuses on quality photos so entering this platform means dedicating some time and thought to your campaign. Through Flickr you can create albums of photos and purchase on demand wall art and photo books to enhance your customers' experience in your establishment.

Based on everything we've covered the idea of tackling a social media marketing campaign head on sounds daunting. The truth is that it can be. Here's what I recommend:

- Start with one platform and master it. Facebook is a great platform to start with because it is what most people are already familiar with and it is very easy to get up and running. Wait until you have a complete page before telling everyone and focus on building a fan base that is engaged, not just pressing like and moving on.

- Once you have a Facebook page with some fans branch out. Take what you have learned and apply it (as much as is applicable) to Twitter or Instagram. I like jumping to Twitter next but Instagram makes sense too as it is essentially an extension of Facebook. The decision is yours but a word of advice: if your demographic trends between thirty and fifty Twitter might be a better choice. If it trends younger than thirty Instagram is probably a better choice.

- If there's any Google products you do use, develop your Places profile to improve your search results ranking and start a YouTube channel. If you use YouTube for nothing else it is an easy video uploader and the embed function is a real asset.

- Remember to track your progress against goals and always be thinking of the future.

- Always conduct yourself with the utmost integrity. Shady dealings or cut corners inevitably become exposed and negative brand perception can spread like wildfire across the Internet. Remember that if you collect email addresses or personal information your customers have trusted you with that info. Do not violate their trust.

- Remember to look to your competitors regularly. Imitating their good ideas and learning from their mistakes is a zero risk proposition for you and can keep them on their toes. If they have a strong presence on a channel that you're not on, look at the possible benefits of expanding your campaign there too.

What Not to Do

Having an understanding of what to do is just as important as understanding pitfalls to avoid. If you do any of the following, or have already done them the world isn't over. Almost everything can be saved and at the end of the day if you learning from your mistakes is a key component of growing.

- Don't **tackle every platform at once. Your efforts will become divided and your brand will lose its consistency and unified** voice.

- Don't **run a social media marketing campaign without planning and goals. Progress tracking is the truest measure of a program's effectiveness.**

- Don't **use your social media channels for personal use. This is a distraction from the purpose of your business efforts and can compromise the integrity of your brand.**

- Don't **assume that because you built a Facebook page and a Twitter profile that you can walk away. Social media campaigns require input and labor to maintain them.**

- Don't **slander your competitors and don't harass, embarrass, or snub people who leave bad reviews or publically make negative statements. While it isn't possible to make every situation right, make a public (if possible) effort to apologize and show your followers that you are listening and that you put your customers first.**

- Don't **forget to build personal relationships with your fans, followers, and customers. It is** *social* **media after all!**

Wrapping it All Up

Thanks for sticking with me the entire time. The Internet is an inconceivably large place populated by an inconceivably large number of people. The statistics just don't do it justice. It is now possible to reach more people than ever before in record time. And not just reach people, but the right people. Building a better understanding of how social media works, how it can be leveraged, and how profitable it really is can help elevate your business to new heights. After taking it all in, I'm sure the question you're asking yourself is "Dang. Why didn't I think of Facebook?"

There is a wealth of information of developing your social media channels available and new information is being released all of the time to fit the ever-changing face of social media today. I hope that this book serves as an anchor for you as you navigate your business through the turbulent waters we find ourselves in.

You've worked hard to get where you are today. I don't have to tell you that there's always more work on the horizon. A well-maintained and carefully planned social media campaign can give you more bang for your buck and hopefully take a little bit of the load off your shoulders. Until next time, thanks for reading, thanks for making delicious food, and never forget to support your local businesses.

Appendix

List of Content

Content that Entertains

- **Quizzes**
- **Competitions**
- **Virals (such as memes, videos, or photos)**
- **Games**
- **Branded entertainment videos**

Content that Inspires

- **Celebrity or thought leader endorsements**
- **Community Forum**
- **Reviews**
- **Articles**
- **Recipes**

Content that Educates

- **Infographics**
- **Press releases**
- **Guides**
- **Trend and graph reporting**
- **Statistics summaries**
- **Informative Articles**

- E-books

- Wikis

- Demo Videos

Content that Convinces

- Ratings

- Case Studies

- Product features or spec sheets

- Checklists

- Pricing guides

- Calculations

- Webinars or presentations

- Reports and white papers

While all of these may not be directly applicable to your business, understanding where each type of content falls can help develop creative solutions to the question "What can I post to start a conversation and get my brand noticed?"

List of Common Measurable Social Media Metrics

- Bounce Rate

- Click-Throughs

- Comments

- Contest Entries

- Conversions

- CPM

- Downloads

- E-book Downloads

- Email Subscribers/unsubscribes

- Facebook Fans
- Favorites
- Geographic Distribution of brand mentions
- Growth Rate of Fans
- Inbound Links
- Leads Generated
- Likes
- Newsletter Subscribers/unsubscribes
- Online Conversations
- Page Views
- Ratings
- Reviews
- Sentiment (positive/negative) associated with your brand
- Social Bookmarks
- Twitter Followers
- Uploads
- User-participation in online polls
- Viral Status of content

Remember that taking in as much information as possible can quickly obscure the true progress of a social media campaign.

Glossary

Brand Magnetism – **The quality or characteristic that a popular brand has in attracting customers based on the brand perception and market position. Brands with high magnetism naturally attract customers who want to be associated with the brand's image.**

CLV – **Customer lifetime value. The amount of revenue generated from a single customer over the lifetime of his or her relationship with your brand.**

Content Curator – **A person who accumulates and maintains different collections of (mostly) value-added content. This "one-stop-shop" approach is a huge benefit to consumers but administrators should beware that it is time-consuming and can be a distraction.**

GIF – **Graphics Interchange Format (pronounced "jiff"). A lossless format for image files that supports both animated and static images.**

Geotag – **A characteristic of a post or photo that contains the coordinates (latitude and longitude) of a photo to place it on a map.**

Meme – **A humorous content parcel (video, image, blog post etc...) that is rapidly shared across the Internet.**

ROI – **Return on investment. A measure of the profitability of campaigns, projects, and undertakings. ROI reporting is an essential component of understanding the effect of social media marketing efforts.**

SEO – **Search engine optimization. SEO consists of various methods of boosting the ranking of your entry in search results such as adding content, links, and keywords.**

Thought leader – **A thought leader is someone who is a "go-to" personality in their field. A thought leader may exist in a large context as in the thought leader for innovation in the tech sector. Alternatively a thought leader could be a local celebrity in a smaller context. In either context people give weight to the opinions of someone they consider to be a thought leader.**

Touch point – **A point of contact with a customer via any of your marketing channels (contemporary or traditional). Generally speaking, the more touch points you have with customers, the more present you are in their minds and more likely they are to patronize your business. The** decision to buy is a complex one that takes many different aspects into account.

Viral – a content parcel that is shared rapidly across the web with extremely high views in a short period of time. At date of publish there is no specific number that denotes content as viral. Non-scientific estimates place the condition of 5 million plus views in a 3-7 day period.

To find out more, or to get personalized help with your bar or restaurant marketing, go to my website, www.BarRestaurantGuru.com.

-Ryan Gougeon